Portraits

9/86 Frelett 9.55

Portraits

Biography and Autobiography
in the Secondary School

Margaret Fleming and Jo McGinnis, Editors
University of Arizona

National Council of Teachers of English
1111 Kenyon Road, Urbana, Illinois 61801

NCTE Editorial Board: Julie M. Jensen, Delores Lipscomb, John S. Mayher, Elisabeth McPherson, John C. Maxwell, *ex officio,* Paul O'Dea, *ex officio*

Staff Editor: Lee Erwin

Book Design: Tom Kovacs for TGK Design

NCTE Stock Number: 36486

Library of Congress Cataloging in Publication Data
Main entry under title:

Portraits: biography and autobiography in the
   secondary school.

   Bibliography: p.
   1. American literature—Study and teaching (Secondary)
—Addresses, essays, lectures. 2. Biography (as a
literary form)—Study and teaching—Addresses, essays,
lectures. 3. Autobiography—Study and teaching—
Addresses, essays, lectures. I. Fleming, Margaret.
II. McGinnis, Jo, 1940–
PS42.P6 1985   810'.7'1273   85-2917
ISBN 0-8141-3648-6

Contents

Preface   vii

Introduction   x

1 Approaches to Biography and Autobiography in the Classroom

Approaches to Biography and Autobiography
in the Classroom   3
   Margaret Fleming

Ourselves and Others: A Sociological Approach   7
   Teresa Link, Lindley Hunter Silverman, and Jo McGinnis

Biography as Art: A Formal Approach   14
   Elizabeth Robertson and Jo McGinnis

Inner Views: A Psychological Approach   22
   Jo McGinnis

Then and Now: A Historical Approach   30
   Nora Bellmann, Sandra Johnson Treharne,
   and Lindley Hunter Silverman

Ideals and Ideas: A Moral/Philosophical Approach   40
   Margaret Fleming

From the Inside Out: A Linguistic Approach   56
   Jo McGinnis

The Power of Myth: An Archetypal Approach   68
   Margaret Fleming

Persona and Persuasion: A Rhetorical Approach   78
   Sandra Johnson Treharne

2 More Ideas for Using Biography and Autobiography

Judging a Book by Its Cover: A Prereading Book Analysis   89
    Jo McGinnis

Dealing with Sensitive Subjects   92
    Randall Smith, Margaret Fleming, Jo McGinnis,
    and Lindley Hunter Silverman

Writing Assignments Focusing on Autobiographical
and Biographical Topics   95
    Margaret Fleming

The Biography Kit   98
    Lindley Hunter Silverman

Bibliography   103

Preface

This book is the result of a somewhat unusual collaboration, although collaboration is by no means unusual. All you have to do to verify that fact is check the bookshelf nearest you or leaf through a current periodical. Ironically, in school we usually insist that writing be a purely individual task, that students rely solely on their own resources, when experienced writers both inside and outside academe are not ashamed to pool their talents.

The benefits of collaboration are obvious. Like any shared task, it lightens the load for each participant while improving the quality of the product. Moreover, the process can be incredibly stimulating, as experience will testify, both my own and that of my colleagues: Jo McGinnis, University of Arizona, Tucson; Lindley Hunter Silverman, Wade Carpenter Junior High School, Nogales, Arizona; Sandra Johnson Treharne, Lubbock Independent Public Schools, Lubbock, Texas; Elizabeth B. Robertson, San Pasqual Valley Unified High School, Winterhaven, California; Randall Smith, Townsend Junior High School, Tucson, Arizona; Teresa Link, University of Arizona, Tucson; and Nora Bellmann, Townsend Junior High School, Tucson, Arizona.

Our collaboration is unusual in that our work is not divided into eight individual chunks but is the result of a much more fluid interaction; therefore, assigning authorial responsibility is difficult. The idea of writing a book grew out of a graduate workshop I recently taught at the University of Arizona. Its topic, "Teaching Biography and Autobiography," was chosen partly because of my own interest in these genres and partly because I wanted to remedy their general neglect in literary study. One symptom of this neglect is that I could not find a text on teaching biography and autobiography; nor could I find much attention devoted to this topic in any of the several texts on teaching literature that I examined.

The seven teachers enrolled in the course were teaching or had taught at junior high, high school, and college levels. They were all gifted—gifted as teachers, as students, as writers, as individuals. I felt fortunate; such a class is rare in any teacher's experience. About halfway through the course I found myself thinking that all this outstanding writing and teaching talent ought to be channeled to reach a wider audience. Perhaps because I had no real doubt that the workshop participants would accept, I hesitated before proposing to them that we collaborate in writing a book on teaching biography and autobiography. I had been there before with *Teaching the Epic* (Urbana, Ill.: NCTE, 1974), and I knew how much work would be involved. Of course, I also knew how exciting it could be. Excitement finally won out over reluctance, and, as I had known they would, the others eagerly accepted the challenge to write the book. Together we reconstructed the rest of the course to that end. In the best tradition of process-oriented writing, we decided that our first task should be to generate lots of material. Organizing, shaping, and revising could all come later.

By the end of the semester, we had generated much of the raw material for our manuscript. The next semester Jo, Lindley, and I began working to edit it, a demanding task but an exhilarating one. We met regularly to discuss and revise and rewrite. I looked forward to these sessions, almost resenting other tasks that took time from this one. The three of us worked well together; we were able to criticize and accept criticism without feeling personally threatened, and we found that our different strengths and weaknesses complemented each other. We became a team, depending on and profiting from each other's advice for everything we wrote. For instance, even though my voice is speaking here, Jo and Lindley have also participated in the writing of this preface. (So has my husband, a constant collaborator.)

Because we did not finish as soon as anticipated (does one ever?), Jo and I found ourselves the next semester without Lindley, who had completed her degree and taken a full-time teaching job in Nogales. Fortunately we were able to recruit Sandy Treharne to work with us for a time. Again, we worked effectively and enjoyably together and—most important—were able to finish our project.

Or so we believed. (Does one ever finish?) When we had sent our manuscript off to NCTE, we thought that all we had to do was wait for an answer. But instead of the yes or no we expected, NCTE reviewers (the Secondary Section, the Commission on Literature, and the Editorial Board) voted to publish the book but made a number of suggestions for expanding and improving it. By this time Jo and I were the only ones available of the original eight. We did the final revising and editing, incorporating the reviewers' suggestions, which we believe have made this a much better book than it would otherwise have been.

This experience has been immensely rewarding to me and, I feel sure, to all the others who have worked on the project (including, I hope, the anonymous NCTE reviewers). I know of no better way to develop collegial rapport than to collaborate in this way. A piece of writing is inevitably enriched by the contributions of different minds and polished by the discussions of organization and style that accompany revision. Collaboration is a strategy for learning writing that might well be fostered in our students. To treat writing as a solitary, individual act may well be to overlook resources that can make it less painful for many and more fruitful for all.

Margaret Fleming

Introduction

Kelly looked stunned. I had told her as gently as I could that, no, Ernest J. Gaines's *The Autobiography of Miss Jane Pittman* (New York: Bantam, 1972) was not a real autobiography, that it was fiction. There was no actual Jane Pittman. Kelly protested that it wasn't possible—the story had seemed so real. Since we had been discussing the differences between fiction and nonfiction in class, it seemed important that a distinction be made, but tears came to her eyes as she struggled to regain composure. I changed the subject and carried on with my seventh-grade English class. As I thought about it later, I realized that the life story of a real person, as Jane Pittman seemed to Kelly, can mean a great deal to a student, whether the story is in the form of biography or autobiography.

Teachers who love to read biography and autobiography themselves need little persuasion to use such selections as literature in the English classroom. They have an intuitive feeling that the life story of a real person can be more powerful than that of any fictional character. Yet to justify replacing a classic work of fiction in the literature curriculum requires more than hazy intuition; it requires a clear sense of what to look for in making a selection, what to aim for as possibilities, and what to expect as results.

Like good fiction, the best biographies and autobiographies are works of art, adhering to the same standards of form. They contain a plot or story line, whether it is, as in Sandburg's three-volume biography of Abraham Lincoln, a line extending from before Lincoln's birth to his death, or, as in Maya Angelou's *I Know Why the Caged Bird Sings,* an autobiographical narrative focusing on incidents in the life of a child and emerging young woman. There are characters and settings to examine, conflicts to unravel, themes and styles of writing to analyze. Like good fiction, biographies and autobiographies describe common shared experiences: birth, the search for identity, coming to terms with sexuality, intellectual growth, social adjustment, career development, and eventual death. Like fiction, they illustrate with colorful language and concrete imagery the details that make the subject's life unique. And because students and their teachers have certain qualitative expectations of the literature they read, a biography or autobiography must above all be good writing.

We make further demands on writers of real-life stories, however. Not only must the material be well written, but it must be historically accurate. Students read all literature to discover truth of some kind: in mysteries, they demand to know the clues, the material circumstances of the crime; in manuals, they read to find out how to do something; in biographical and historical writing, they want first to know what happened. While biographies are sources for more than historical truth, any good biography should furnish a background of the world and times of the subject, because no one lives in a historical vacuum.

Techniques of style and an appropriate background are as necessary for good biography and autobiography as they are for fiction, but, as in a portrait painting, style and setting only enhance the portrayal of the subject. The development of character is the primary focus. Because students want to care about what happens in the life of the person they read about, whether real or fictional, they demand that the real-life subject above everything else be an interesting person. Teachers can depend on an insatiable human curiosity about the affairs of other people to get students interested initially, but that interest must be sustained once the story is begun. That sustained interest often depends upon which details of a person's life are highlighted and which others are de-emphasized or glossed over. Choice of representative detail in turn often depends upon the author's purpose for writing and the book's intended audience. Biography and autobiography separate into two distinct, if similar, genres at this point.

Biography has a long history of use in educating young people, and the purposes and ways of portraying a life in words and then of using that account to teach students have changed over the centuries. One of our oldest forms of literature, the heroic poem, was a kind of fictionalized biography, and recording the accomplishments of great men was probably the first historical writing. If we can assume that the primary purpose of this written work was to entertain listeners or to set down a historical record, another traditional use of biography was to provide inspiration and example for listeners and readers. The anecdotes of Plutarch's *Lives,* for example, were, as Barbara Tuchman explains in *Telling Lives,* "designed to delight and edify the reader while at the same time inculcating ethical principles." These three objectives are still at the top of a longer list of reasons for writing biography and using it in the classroom. However, teachers who demand entertaining, edifying, value-oriented biography for their students should be aware of the potential abuse of each of these characteristics.

To delight student audiences is a worthy goal, yet biographers who have entertainment as their primary purpose are tempted, like the tellers of heroic tales, to amplify the story, enhancing it to heroic proportions and straying into the realm of fiction. An uncertain boundary often separates fictional literature and the nonfiction of biography, and explaining the difference, especially to a young reader completely caught up in the life portrayed, can be difficult.

It becomes even more difficult when the work purports to "edify" its audience, to be an authentic, historically accurate representation of a life story. Even biographies written with honest intentions fall short of the whole truth, primarily because of the difficulties of choosing the representative details in a person's life. If, however, teachers are careful to present biography—and autobiography—as interpretation of fact, as merely one person's version of the truth, then searching for truths found in biography—psychological, philosophical, and sociological, as well as historical—becomes an educational opportunity and challenge. Comparing the biographer's truth to the version of truth in standard works of history involves a historical approach. The considerations of point of view, persona, audience, and message suggest a rhetorical approach.

The intention of biography to "inculcate ethical principles" is another worthy goal that can go too far, resulting in bad teaching as well as bad biography. When Parson Weems inserted the apocryphal story of George Washington chopping down a cherry tree to illustrate the honesty and good character of our nation's hero, his intentions were no doubt good, but it wasn't good biography. A moral and philosophical approach that attempts to analyze values represented in the text is worthwhile, but readers may resist a biography that preaches too much or that overstates its eulogy to a departed hero.

Traditionally, biographies were testimonials to the deeds and accomplishments—the public life—of a great person. Unfortunately, the result was often what Mark Twain called "but the clothes and buttons" of the subject. At its best the characterization was one-dimensional; at its worst the treatment tended to glorify the warrior hero, ignoring the unpleasant motives and consequences of conquest. Lytton Strachey wrote what is now considered the first of the modern biographies, presenting a more balanced approach to lives of eminent Victorians. The "new" biographies since Strachey have probed for the personality behind the public poses. Not only is the prose more readable, but the deeper character development and the study of psychological motivation lend new perspectives to biographical writing, suggesting potential classroom uses beyond the original objectives of entertainment, edification, and ethics.

The new biographies are multifaceted, three-dimensional portrayals of subjects who are less paragons of moral virtue than humans much like ourselves. The old biographies often traced the life history of a subject as one clear path of cause and effect, a single-minded quest for greatness. The new biographies often show the more realistic qualities of ambiguity, ambivalence, and indecision. When biographers concentrate less on the later successful lives of their subjects and more on the struggles, hopes, disappointments, conflicts, and dreams of the earlier years of childhood and adolescence, students find parallels with their own lives and are more willing to identify with the subjects.

Autobiographies differ in many respects from biographies; they too have changed in use and purpose over the years. Early autobiographers wrote for many different reasons, as they generally carefully explain in their works. Often they wrote to satisfy the requests of their children or friends or to create a record that would recount history as they saw it. The same general reasons for reading and teaching biography—as entertainment, edification, and example—also apply to autobiography. The new autobiographies, however, seem more often to be written in order to gather together memories that create a pattern explaining the shape one's life has taken. Autobiographers still seem to want to explain history from a personal point of view, but instead of the recurring image of a great man looking back over his life, calmly recalling his accomplishments and his triumphs over adversity, the new autobiographies reveal more vulnerability and personal voice.

This intensely personal voice is the fundamental difference between autobiography and biography, and that voice has advantages for teachers as well as disadvantages. The first-person "I" voice invites more intimacy than does the third-person "he" or "she," making it easier for students to identify with the subjects, to care about what happened in their lives. Yet the third-person voice in biography can represent a more consistent, if not necessarily objective, viewpoint. As the rhetorical analysis of *I Know Why the Caged Bird Sings* shows (see "Persona and Persuasion: A Rhetorical Approach"), the "I" voice in autobiography undergoes a rhetorical change from the "I" writing at the present moment to the "I" who experienced something as a child. The potential for objectivity is possibly greater in biography because of the view from the outside *into* the personality. The viewpoint from the inside outward in autobiography is necessarily subjective. Because biographers must rely on verifiable data to reconstruct a life, the demand and thus the potential for historical accuracy (in terms of the outer world of the subject) is great. It is far more difficult to question or verify the autobiographer's personal feelings and viewpoints.

Biographies have a certain advantage over autobiographies in their predictable form. Biographical writing follows, generally, certain conventions of writing, reconstructing a life from childhood to death, or to the present time, if the subject is still living. Biographies often make some statement of the influence that person has had on society and summarizes his or her life accomplishments. While an autobiography cannot, obviously, treat one's death and the subsequent influence of one's life, autobiographical writing in its "pure" form is an overview of one's life from childhood to the present. Yet autobiographical writing has a far more flexible format than biography. Journals, essays, and letters are not true autobiography, but they too are rich resources to stimulate interest in a person's life, especially in regard to the lives of women, who more often wrote privately than publicly. Autobiographical writing may include only parts of one's life, as in the Watergate-era books by John Dean and others, or *In Search of History,* by Theodore White.

Biography and autobiography differ in another fundamental respect: autobiographers need not be "famous" people if they can write an interesting story in a compelling way. Maya Angelou's writing is what made an otherwise interesting but generally unknown life one that has come to represent the southern black woman, suggesting that autobiography can offer people who might otherwise be excluded by the dominant culture a way to voice their experiences. Another advantage is that students are more likely to identify with a writer who has not been elevated by a biographer to hero status.

Once students have identified with a subject, either in a biography or autobiography, a teacher can feel confident that not only has the reading experience been valuable for them, but that they have made an essential step forward in education. Psychological development in all children must eventually include some realization that other people and other cultures exist in the world, each representing the center of a personal or social universe, a cosmos. That realization may come as a shock to some young people who live in a normally self-centered world, yet finding out that the complex interior life we carry around with us is duplicated—yet differently so—in other people has a double benefit. Good biographies and autobiographies not only nudge young people into an awareness of others' existence in the universe, thus widening their horizons, but also remind them that they are not alone in their problems.

Most important to the teacher of English in a writing-centered classroom is that writing assignments are natural outgrowths of and preparations for the reading. Students can respond to passages in an autobiography with their own experiences, using examples from the model they are reading. They may respond in writing to questions that will be discussed in the reading. Biographies can stimulate serious biographical research or experiments with historical fiction or modern mythology. Because students should become aware that one cannot depend solely upon biography to learn history, teachers may assign work that encourages comparison and contrast of sources. The "Applications" section at the end of each chapter and the suggestions for writing assignments in section 2 offer other possibilities.

Selecting a suitable biography or autobiography is not an easy task. Texts that meet the standards for good writing and historical accuracy, and that portray an interesting subject with depth and a balanced sense of commitment and purpose, simply are not available in great numbers. Fortunately, there is help for teachers who may be overwhelmed by the responsibility. The bibliography on pages 103–4 includes several lists of biographical works suitable for young people. In addition, Kenneth Donelson and Alleen Pace Nilsen's *Literature for Today's Young Adults* includes a checklist for evaluating biography, as well as a collection of biographical titles.

Nothing will replace good fiction in the literature curriculum, but fine work in biography and autobiography exists as an exciting alternative. While both may be taught in the same ways as fiction, other approaches are available as well, depending upon the educational objectives in mind. The problem of determining the differences between fact and fiction, or between fact and the interpretation of fact, cannot be denied, but it can be turned to advantage. Helping students first to see the problem and then to find answers may be a way to help them move out of the world of character and plot in fiction and into a new world of ideas in nonfiction.

Jo McGinnis

1 Approaches to Biography and Autobiography in the Classroom

Approaches to Biography and Autobiography in the Classroom

Margaret Fleming

When I was a beginning teacher the most difficult part of teaching literature for me was asking questions that would challenge my students to think. My experience as an educator has convinced me that I was not unique, that the ability to ask probing questions is an art developed by long practice. Yet there may be shortcuts. In those early days, I took great comfort from remembering *plot, character, setting,* and *theme.* Basing my questions on these four aspects gave me confidence that I had, in some sense, "covered" the work in question.

In later years I expanded my repertoire of heuristics for asking questions. Bloom's taxonomy has proved useful for any subject, especially for generating questions at higher levels of thinking than mere recall. Aristotle's *topics* are also useful generally, and his triad of *speaker, subject,* and *audience* is relevant for rhetorical analysis. Burke's *pentad* is similar to the plot-character-setting-theme quartet but easier for some students to grasp. The idea of using formal, moral/philosophical, psychological, historical, and archetypal approaches was suggested by Wilfred Guerin et al. in *A Handbook of Critical Approaches to Literature.* In my methods courses for literature, I have used these very successfully, adding sociological and linguistic approaches, which provide additional dimensions. Most recently, I have discovered Kohlberg's stages of moral development as a heuristic.

This book, then, incorporates many of these ways of structuring questions and activities for the study of literature. They are meant to be suggestive only, not exhaustive. For instance, we would not want to imply that Freud's model is the only way to approach literature psychologically or that Kohlberg's stages have a monopoly on moral perspectives. For beginning teachers, the guidelines included in each chapter may be useful as a sort of checklist for planning discussion and activities; experienced teachers will be able to use them more eclectically, incorporating ideas into their own teaching strategies.

While of course these strategies can be used with any work of literature, we have chosen to focus on biography and autobiography for two reasons. First, these genres, and nonfiction in general, receive much less attention in literary curricula and in books on teaching literature than does so-called imaginative literature. So, while English teachers have a wealth of strategies to choose from when studying fiction, poetry, and drama, they may be at a loss when it comes to nonfiction. Second, biography and autobiography may profitably be studied across the curriculum. History teachers, for example, often use these genres to "bring to life" the events recounted in textbooks, to give students a feel for the culture of a particular time and place.

Literature teachers thus will be likely to find formal, moral/philosophical, rhetorical, linguistic, and archetypal approaches most congenial, since they concentrate on the text itself. Teachers of social studies, whose main interest is not text, but context, may prefer sociological, psychological, and historical approaches, although these can also help illuminate literature if they are used in a way that does not detract from it.

The chapters in this section, then, represent eight different critical approaches to literature, used with two representative works: *Abe Lincoln Grows Up,* by Carl Sandburg, and *I Know Why the Caged Bird Sings,* by Maya Angelou. Although the structures of the chapters vary because different people contributed to different approaches, each chapter includes an explanation of one approach and an analysis of one of the two works, using the approach specified. This analysis is meant to give teachers an idea of the sort of insights to be gained from that particular approach to the work. In addition, each chapter includes general guidelines for using the approach with any work of biography or autobiography and a section of applications that suggests classroom projects, questions for discussion, and possible writing assignments. While most of the applications are related directly to the work analyzed, teachers may infer from them the sorts of applications that might apply to another work.

The chapters dealing with the formal approach and the moral/philosophical approach are different from the others in format, the former because of its familiarity to teachers and the latter because of its possible unfamiliarity. Because the analysis of literature on the basis of its *form*— the plot, characters, setting, and theme—is the traditional and familiar approach to literature in the English classroom, the "fable" that begins "Biography as Art: A Formal Approach" describes a classroom in which students learn, through discussing, comparing, and analyzing, that ways to look at fiction may be applied as well to nonfiction like biography and autobiography. While no student discussion proceeds as smoothly as in this mythical classroom (hence "fable"), the story illustrates an ideal of group discussion and inductive learning.

Similarly, "Ideals and Ideas: A Moral/Philosophical Approach," possibly the most unfamiliar and intimidating (to the teacher) of these approaches to literature, begins with a model discussion in the teachers' lounge. There, the model teacher confidently and persuasively justifies and explains an approach that might cause misgivings among teachers, administrators, and parents.

In a graduate seminar or workshop like the one that generated this text, approaching the same work from eight different directions inevitably deepens understanding of it, forcing examination of aspects that might not come to mind otherwise. In a secondary school classroom, a less structured strategy is recommended, the teacher selecting—from the wealth of possible questions generated—whatever might be appropriate for the level of interest and sophistication of a particular class.

Our choice of the two works to use as examples was guided by several specific criteria and a bit of serendipity as well. We wanted to choose one autobiography and one biography, both excellent examples of their genres. We also wanted subjects—one male and one female—who were worth knowing about. Neither of these works portrays the subject's entire life, each being part of a series, but we thought that the early years—up through adolescence—might have more immediate appeal to secondary school students than the whole life, and we came increasingly to believe that both these books are easy enough for younger students to read but sophisticated enough for use with older ones as well. Serendipity presented us with a white and a black American as subjects, a statesman and an artist, and a nineteenth- and a twentieth-century figure.

We anticipated no objection to the biography of Lincoln, but we hesitated over Angelou's autobiography because of her forthright treatment of racial and sexual topics. Eventually, however, we decided that the advantages of using her book outweighed the disadvantages, and, furthermore, that confronting potential problems was a better policy than avoiding them; we address this issue more specifically in section 2. A number of books are available from NCTE on censorship and avoiding problems in this regard.

Some might object that analyzing any work of literature so systematically will rob it of its primary affective quality, but this is one of the challenges of teaching literature. While the emphasis in this book is cognitive, we do not underrate literature's affective qualities. A reader's response is crucial; it is the first step toward understanding. What we do here is not meant to replace that experience but to take it one step further. Choosing a passage for analysis that students find particularly appealing or memorable will help ensure that questions will build on and add to an already enthusiastic response to the literature. By increasing intellectual understanding, we hope to lead readers to a fuller emotional response, so that ultimately both kinds of understanding are fused in a true aesthetic experience.

Ourselves and Others:
A Sociological Approach

Teresa Link, Lindley Hunter Silverman, and Jo McGinnis

Through food we learned that there were other people in the world.

—*I Know Why the Caged Bird Sings*

We all have memories. Yet often they lie dormant until something new in our experience awakens them. This revival of memory is the very essence of autobiographical writing, which then triggers links between our lives and the life we are reading about. The exploration of these links can be dynamically enhanced by a sociological analysis of literature.

This useful approach calls upon our general knowledge of common cultural traits: what we eat, what we wear, where we live, and so on. Because these traits are familiar to all students, classroom discussion is animated and spontaneous; a high percentage of participation is guaranteed, providing that the classroom climate invites everyone's contribution and encourages differing opinion. Besides its emphasis on concrete items and specific details, the sociological approach gives value to students' personal experience, allowing even the poorest readers to tackle the reading assignments on their own.

Given that the approach is so immediately accessible to a broad range of students, we should remind ourselves to make full use of the questioning power that rests in the approach. A full taxonomy of levels of questioning, as set out by Benjamin Bloom et al. in *Taxonomy of Educational Objectives: Handbook 1: Cognitive Domain,* should be the scaffolding for a full-blown discussion. Not only is it important to include all six levels of questioning for discussion, but also it is important to progress systematically through one level of questioning to the next. The examples that follow are based on Maya Angelou's *I Know Why the Caged Bird Sings,* using one of the most obvious and immediately appealing topics for discussion: food.

Aromatic, mouth-watering descriptions pepper Angelou's text; she appeals to our taste buds, as in the following excerpt, the focus of this analysis and series of questions:

> On Sunday mornings Momma served a breakfast that was geared to
> hold us quiet from 9:30 a.m. to 3:00 p.m. She fried thick pink slabs
> of home-cured ham and poured the grease over sliced red tomatoes.
> Eggs over easy, fried potatoes and onions, yellow hominy and crisp
> perch fried so hard we would pop them in our mouths and chew
> bones, fins and all. Her cathead biscuits were at least three inches in
> diameter and two inches thick. (30)

Ordinarily questioning starts at the *knowledge* level (and too frequently
does not go beyond). For example, a teacher might ask the class to
contribute to a list of what Maya ate for breakfast on Sunday mornings.
Not only does such a question require accurate and specific response; it
draws attention to the passage. Students should be encouraged to consult
their texts, citing the page and paragraph for the benefit of everyone's
attention. This level of questioning trains students early to *use their books*
and to support their ideas with evidence from the text.

To stay at level one, and even level two, would contribute to a
deadening "workbook" approach to teaching, but the two levels are
essential for informally testing whether students have read and understood
the material. The second level of questioning is for *comprehension.* Here
the question might be, "What do you think Angelou means by 'Momma
served a breakfast that was *geared to hold us quiet*'?" Students respond
on this level in their own words, and this requires some personal grasp of
the material. Not only is it important to see if the words mean the same
thing to all students, but it helps students to distinguish their way of
expressing ideas from Angelou's. Even in this short passage we begin to
see that breakfast is more than simply a menu.

Joining what they know of Maya's Sunday breakfast with their own
memories of breakfast moves the class to the third level of questioning:
application. This level relies on previously learned information, that
reservoir of experience that students bring to the reading act. Here
teachers purposefully solicit various and diverse observations "On Breakfast," which serve as the basis for an interpretation of the cultural importance of food. In a class that emphasizes frequent informal writing,
students may respond to writing assignments designed to draw on personal experience, opinion, and/or knowledge of how other people in the
world think of breakfast. The assignment possibilities are varied: writing
about "ritual" breakfasts; favorite breakfasts, from no breakfast at all,
thank you, or cold leftover pizza, to elaborate ethnic feasts; or sensory
details of a remembered childhood breakfast for comparison with
Angelou's. A sorting and classifying exercise is appropriate at this level,
possibly drawing on knowledge students bring to the classroom from
other areas; for example, what different cultures or different parts of the
country are represented in Maya's menu? This level of questioning is

exciting in discussion or in sharing of writing; a great wealth of personal experience and memory floods the classroom, perhaps even to the point of saturation. When so deluged, the class will need to return to the text to re-examine it with fresh insight. Teachers can help students avoid a possibly sensitive subject by wording the assignments and questions so that more impersonal contributions are as acceptable as personal experience. The writer's voice, for example, may speak in the third person, describing a "friend."

The fourth level—*analysis*—may be threatening to both the student and the teacher, because analytical questions can elicit several different answers, all potentially correct. Moreover, the entire tempo of the discussion changes. What has become a lively exchange may begin to fade. Often there are lapses between comments or, worse, no comments at all. Critical thinking takes time and effort. Students attempt to identify the motives behind Momma's Sunday breakfasts, generalizing about those motives and giving evidence to support or refute the generalizations. Momma, for example, holds strong religious beliefs that both confuse and amuse Maya. Detailed discussion may lead to an awareness that perhaps Momma's reason for serving such a substantial meal is to glorify the bounty of the Lord and to impress the visiting preacher. We encounter at this level of questioning the constant temptation to be lured from one topic of discussion—food—to another: religion. These shifts highlight how different sociological aspects may interact.

The writing-oriented teacher may ask students to respond to the question in writing, so that the period of silence helps them to focus on an answer. Teachers working with small discussion groups may get more response if each group is asked to list as many motives as they can think of and report to the general group their results. A receptive attitude on the part of the teacher will encourage students who worry about "wrong" answers to participate in the discussion without fear.

The fifth level of questioning—*synthesis*—combines reading insights and personal experience with the goal of creating an original statement. This level of questioning is highly speculative, based on discoveries of what we have just learned or relearned. If students are asked to imagine, for example, what other people in Maya's community eat for breakfast, they must stretch their minds to search for creative responses to and possible partial solutions for complex social problems. For example, the passage may serve as a point of departure for considering a world where people may eat only one meal a day, or where some people eat and many go hungry.

The use of Bloom's taxonomy has moved students some distance from the preparatory knowledge-level question listing Maya's breakfast delights. It has also moved them away from the text, but *evaluation,* the last level of questioning, can return them to it, involving their abilities to judge all that has been generated in the discussion to this point. Students are asked to evaluate eating habits and eating preferences to see what they tell us about ourselves and people in the literature we read. Only at this level, after having progressed through the previous five levels, are students prepared at last to comment meaningfully on why they like or dislike the book, because their comments have some legitimate force of argument rather than vague and unexamined personal opinion. Subjective criticism and aesthetic appreciation compel the students to establish some criteria for judging effective writing, either by means of a personal set of values or some objective standards. For example, students may determine that food can be used effectively in writing to advance the plot, to establish the setting, and to suggest traits of character, that sensory descriptions of food are part of an effective style. Assignments that encourage students to use their new standards in original writing are appropriate after the discussion is finished. For example, in an outside project, students might volunteer to do the family grocery shopping and to observe what people put into their carts. In a character sketch of one of the shoppers they observe, they may speculate how many members are in the family, what their ages are, and what they eat for a typical breakfast (or other meal). Is someone in the family on a diet? Does the cook in the family enjoy cooking? Are there small children? In students' writing, the emphasis should be on food and what it tells their readers about the characters they are describing, using Angelou's writing as a model.

The beauty of the sociological approach using Bloom's taxonomy is that it begins so clearly and basically with the text. From this strong starting point, the questions can extend beyond the usual elementary levels of knowledge and comprehension. Angelou's autobiography allows us to savor many rich passages. Her memory is so vividly brought to life in her words that she inspires us to attempt to recall with greater clarity and expression our own memories. But Maya's experience is now ours also, and we can use that experience to pursue our quest to bring order to our chaotic world, balance to our personal lives.

Guidelines for Using the Sociological Approach

1. Select a passage that is particularly memorable and that illustrates some aspect of sociology: food, clothing, housing, economy/work, education, religion, family structure. Or, make lists of instances in which the different categories are mentioned.
2. Construct a series of questions for discussion of this passage or these details, beginning with the lowest level of questioning, *knowl-*

edge, and progressing through successively more challenging levels: *comprehension, application, analysis, synthesis,* and *evaluation.* Each level should build on the knowledge gained at a lower level.

3. Prepare for more than one "correct" answer at the levels above *knowledge* and *comprehension.* Develop a receptive attitude to encourage broad participation in the discussion.

4. Prepare to guide the students back to the text and the subject in question when the class enters a sensitive area or when the discussion gets off the track.

Classroom Applications of "Ourselves and Others: A Sociological Approach"

The following are stimulants for discussion and writing based on Angelou's work, using the sociological approach in conjunction with Bloom's taxonomy of questioning. For each sociological category, examples of possible questions are given, but they do not necessarily build on each other sequentially, as questions will in a structured close analysis of one passage. Rather, varied questions at all levels will suggest different passages to develop a full taxonomy for class discussion. The number of each question corresponds to the number of the level of questioning. For example, 4 will always be an *analysis* question.

Before asking any higher-level question, the teacher or the students will have to formulate lower-level questions that point toward this level. Teachers may assign passages to small groups for them to formulate discussion questions. This activity will provide an opportunity for additional learning and responsibility-sharing, once the levels of questioning have been explained.

Clothing

1. Name four costumes Maya wears on different occasions in her life.

2. Describe in your own words the dress worn at Maya's graduation.

3. Demonstrate how clothes distinguish social class, age, occupation, and different regions of the country by citing evidence from the text.

4. Analyze the importance of the blue serge suit Maya dreams of wearing as a trolley car conductor.

5. Design the costumes for a dramatization of a portion of *I Know Why the Caged Bird Sings.*

6. Judge a man by the clothes he wears, a woman by the clothes she wears, using criteria developed in class discussion of the text.

Housing

1. Enumerate the different homes Maya lives in.
2. Explain the housing situations in Stamps, St. Louis, San Francisco, and Los Angeles, as they appear in the text.
3. Illustrate what it means to live "on the wrong side of the tracks" from Maya's description of Stamps, Arkansas.
4. Differentiate between the "homelike" atmospheres of Momma's store and the Los Angeles junkyard.
5. Construct a layout of Stamps, Arkansas, using distinct geographical features and illustrating with appropriate housing for each section of town, using evidence from the text as far as possible, and your own imagination and possible research for the rest.
6. Assess the positive and negative features of each of Maya's homes.

Economy / Work

1. Name four facts about the Great Depression you learned from reading the text.
2. Describe how the Depression affected life in Stamps.
3. Illustrate the effects of the Depression by interviewing someone who lived through it. Compare that person's experience with Maya's.
4. Debate the statement, "The needs of a society determine its ethics."
5. Formulate a barter system similar to the one in Stamps that might work within the context of today's economic realities.
6. Assess how money (or lack thereof) affects people in Stamps; in our time.

Education

1. Outline Maya's formal education.
2. Describe the teaching styles of Mrs. Flowers, Miss Kirwin, and Daddy Clidell.
3. Demonstrate some differences between what Maya learns from her teachers, her friends, her parents, and her brother. How do these differences compare to your experience?
4. Categorize different types of teachers, including Maya's teachers in the list of types.
5. Propose criteria for a good teacher.
6. Choose three teachers who have influenced you and evaluate their influence.

Religion

1. Relate the "hot" church service scenes in *I Know Why the Caged Bird Sings*.

2. Describe the effect of religion on the lives of the black people of Stamps.

3. Interpret Maya's comment that "of all the needs a lonely child has, the one that must be satisfied . . . is the unshaking need for an unshakable God. My pretty Black brother was my Kingdom Come" (19).

4. Diagram the components of religion that are the same for all the faiths you are familiar with.

5. Relate these quotations to one another:

   a. "All asked the same questions. How long, oh God? How long? How long must we wait to be free?" (111)

   b. "The idea came to me that my people may be a race of masochists and that not only was it our fate to live the poorest, roughest life but that we liked it like that." (102)

6. Evaluate the importance of religion in Maya's life; in America today.

Family Structure

1. Define *matriarchal society* as seen in Angelou's work.

2. Describe how a matriarchal society affects Maya and Bailey.

3. Dramatize an incident not specifically narrated in the text involving an encounter between a child and a parent figure. For example, write a dialogue regarding what happened with Maya, Bailey, Uncle Willie, and Momma after the "hot" church service (32–37).

4. Examine the quotation "like father, like son" or "like mother, like daughter" as it relates to the text.

5. Propose alternative family structures in one of Maya's living situations and construct a plot outline of how her life might have been changed as a result. For example, what if Momma had remarried? What if Mr. Freeman had not been killed?

6. Assess the importance of family structure in *I Know Why the Caged Bird Sings*; in America today.

Biography as Art:
A Formal Approach

Elizabeth Robertson and Jo McGinnis

... while the structure of his bones, the build and hang of his torso and limbs, took shape, other elements, invisible, yet permanent, traced their lines in the tissues of his head and heart.

—*Abe Lincoln Grows Up*

A Fable

Once upon a time there was a literature teacher who was very eager to make her students think about what they read in class. She tried very hard to think of ways to help her students analyze stories. One day she decided to have a contest. She read one chapter from each of two different books to her students. Then she told them that there was a very important reason that the two books were different and that they must try to solve the mystery of what the important difference was. She then divided her class into five groups and said that each group would be allowed only one guess.

All of the groups became engrossed in discussing the two stories, and in a short while one of the groups was ready to make its guess. A student from that group stood up and said, "Only one of the stories used a chronological order in describing the incidents. The narrator in the second story used flashbacks to jump around in the time sequence."

The teacher was very pleased with the answer and went up to the board to write down some terms. All of the students watched closely. The teacher then told the class that the first group's guess was correct information that they would need later on, but that it was not the answer to the puzzle.

Group Two was ready with its answer: "Our group noticed that the characters of the two stories were different. The main character in the first story was just a kid, and in the second story an older person was telling the story. There was a difference in the way the other characters were introduced, too."

Once again the teacher wrote down some terms and smiled at a very good answer—but it still didn't answer the question.

The third group was very excited and chose two people to give the answer they had agreed upon. The first one said, "It's obvious that the settings were different!" The second one added, "There were more places mentioned in the second story, but settings were more detailed and given much more importance in the first."

The teacher was extremely pleased with the thorough answer that this group had given. Again she wrote notes on the board, but sighed and said, "Not yet. Let's hear from the next group."

The fourth group was happy that it still had a chance at the answer. The person selected to speak turned red at having to report to the entire class, but spoke clearly: "There was a definite moral in the first story. All the situations and characters seemed to point to a lesson to be learned. There was no such strong message in the other one."

"Very perceptive indeed!" the teacher exclaimed. And she wrote more on her growing list of notes on the board. Then she turned to respond to the raised hands in Group Five.

The fifth group was grateful that it could share its guess with the class, for its members had analyzed the two stories rather deeply. "As speaker for Group Five," said one member, "I am proud to tell you our conclusions. We observed a considerable difference in the way the stories were written. One seemed very matter-of-fact in tone, and the author used short sentences with simple words. The other one seemed to have an apologetic tone and the sentences . . . Wait a minute! I forgot which was which now." He turned to the rest of the members in his group. "What was it we decided, anyway?" Another member spoke up: "The two chapters that we read clearly represented two different styles of writing. Because style is the way the author uses language to tell the story, a lot of the things that have already been mentioned would contribute to the difference in style."

Oh, the teacher was very pleased! "That was an outstanding answer!" she exclaimed. "It shows that you really thought about something difficult. And remember," she smiled at the embarrassed first speaker who had become confused, "to help you in the future—you may always write down notes when having a group discussion."

All the groups had reported, and the teacher finished making her notes on the board. She turned to the class and said, "Even though you didn't solve the mystery, I want you to know that what you have done is even more useful. You have helped me find a way to make an important observation that involves the answer to the question. Before we talk about that answer, however, let's take a look at what is on the board."

Guidelines for Using the Formal Approach

1. *Plot:* What is the structure and organization of the work? Where is the climax? Where and when does the story begin? Where and when does it end? Does the author give hints during the story line as to the outcome of the plot?

2. *Characters:* Who are the principal characters? How are they introduced and developed? Who is telling the story? How much does that narrator know about the thoughts and the feelings of the characters?

3. *Setting:* In what different settings does the action take place? How fully are they described? How important are the settings to the story?

4. *Theme:* What central idea is explored in the work? Does the title give any clues?

5. *Style:* What is the tone of the work? How much does the author use dialogue, narration, description, reflection? What do the vocabulary and sentence structure tell you about the author, the theme, and the audience?

After the students had had time to think about and discuss the five points listed on the board, one of the students in the front row raised a hand—tentatively. "Wait a minute," she said. "Are these stories true, or are they made up?"

The teacher smiled a secret smile and asked the class, "Well, what do you think, class? Would you say they were fiction or nonfiction?" There was considerable disagreement, and finally the teacher quieted the discussion and said, "That was a very good question to ask, because the answer to it is the solution to our original puzzle. One of the stories—the first—is fiction, and the other is nonfiction. The important thing that I want you to notice is that the five categories on the board work well for both the stories that I read to you. They are a helpful guide for analyzing all kinds of prose narrative, both fiction and nonfiction. We will be studying some examples of nonfiction in the next few weeks in the form of biographies and autobiographies, which are, after all, just another kind of story, a story of some person's life. Write down the five headings for future reference, please. You will be needing them."

When the bell rang, the students were happy to be excused. The teacher had gone a little overboard with her lesson that day, they thought.

The End

To the Reader: If you do not believe that fiction and nonfiction can be used simultaneously for instructional purposes, then reread this fable.

A Formal Analysis of *Abe Lincoln Grows Up*

In writing the biography of Abraham Lincoln, Carl Sandburg divides the chronology of Lincoln's early life into two major parts, which make up the volume entitled *The Prairie Years*. Part 1, which is a book in itself, has been edited for young readers and is titled *Abe Lincoln Grows Up*. As the title suggests, this phase of Lincoln's biography covers the formative years of Abe's life. It begins with a brief ancestral history of Lincoln's paternal grandfather—also named Abraham—and continues through Abe's birth and the first twenty-one years of his life. A special feature of this edition is a series of illustrations resembling woodcuts that depict settlement life and various other aspects of the story. The artist, James Daugherty, vividly captures Sandburg's rustic descriptions in simple but effective form.

The characters described in the work range from Abe's ancestors to his immediate family and others directly involved with him, and Sandburg presents all of them with vivacious candor and authenticity. In particular he writes a moving portrayal of Abe's relationship with his mother, his stepmother, and his father.

Within the structure of the biography, Sandburg introduces noted historical figures significant to those years from 1809 to 1831. In doing this, he incorporates subtle flashback and "flashforward" techniques for figures such as Daniel Boone, Johnny Appleseed, and President Andrew Jackson to enhance the limited information available about the personal life of Abe. Where the lack of historical documentation places restrictions upon the biographer, he enriches the material with the political, cultural, and geographical history of the period. This biography is a product of serious historical research, and Sandburg is careful not to "fictionalize" Abe's life. Dialogue, for example, a staple of fiction, is rarely used in this work. Sandburg explains in a note: "Throughout this work conversational utterances are based word for word on sources deemed authentic" (32).

To provide detail and color without fictionalizing, Sandburg elaborates on the various settings involved in Lincoln's life. There is a vivid description of the Lincoln family migration from Pennsylvania to Kentucky, Indiana, and Illinois. The general movement of the settlers is juxtaposed with the history of Indian uprisings and the politics of the period. Specific local surroundings at Knob Creek Farm, Little Pigeon Creek, Gentryville, and the environs of the Mississippi River, where Lincoln spent his boyhood, receive special emphasis. The richness of the poet-author's own voice dominates throughout the volume, especially in passages commenting upon the culture in which Abe grew up. The sections describing the humor, folk wisdom, and superstitions of the settlers offer particular insight. Rather than distracting from the biography, these passages add valuable perspective to the work.

The actual transitions that Abe experienced with his family in moving from Kentucky to Indiana lend a credible and exciting plot to the story, which includes the tragic death of his mother and his father's eventual remarriage. A natural climax occurs when Abe ventures from home for the first time to make a raft trip down the Mississippi River to New Orleans, where he observes the horrors of the slave trade.

Two general themes dominate this work: the strength needed to survive in the wilderness and the attitudes toward education in the backwoods. There is a tension between the values of Abe's father, who thought "eddication" unnecessary, a waste of time, and his stepmother, who encouraged Abe to go to school.

Sandburg's tone throughout the biography remains consistently that of an enthralling storyteller. His rustic style, created from simple vocabulary, is prose in poetic language. Because of this unique use of simple words, *Abe Lincoln Grows Up* lends itself well to audiences of junior high age, while the style and richness of material make it appropriate for students in high school as well.

Guidelines for Using the Formal Approach

In the preceding fable, a general guide is provided for use in analyzing literature of all kinds, using the formal approach. Below are additional guidelines more specifically directed toward analyzing biography and autobiography. Suggestions for writing assignments are also included.

1. *Plot:* In fictional writing, the plot is often far more tightly drawn than in stories of real people. Instead of one dramatic climax, for example, a biography or autobiography may include several climactic episodes. Draw a "lifeline," showing graphically the peaks and valleys representing significant happenings in the subject's life. The highest peak may represent a kind of natural climax. Experiment with a personal lifeline in the same way to generate autobiographical or biographical writing based upon natural climaxes in your own or another's life.

   Read the beginning paragraphs of *The Catcher in the Rye*, by J. D. Salinger, which pokes fun at autobiographies and at people who write the "typical" autobiography. Discuss the conventions of the genre: How do most autobiographies begin? In what sequence and form is the story written? Compare a "classic" work (Boswell's *Life of Johnson*, for example) with a modern one, or compare a fictionalized work with nonfiction (as in the fable). Compare the beginning paragraphs from several autobiographies (see the Bibliography for recommended works). What makes an effective opening statement for an autobiography? What might you expect from the rest of the book after reading the beginning sentences? Write the beginning paragraph of your own autobiography and compare it (anonymously, if you prefer) with those of other students and with published autobiographies to see how vital information is revealed in the opening statement.

2. *Character:* Whereas the writer of fiction has the advantage of inventing characters and of indicating what is going on in their thoughts, only in autobiography does the reader of nonfiction know what the subject is thinking. In biography, the writer can only infer from the actions of the subject and other characters what might be going on in the person's head. Look for evidence that the biographer is overstepping the bounds of scholarly writing in this respect.

    Who are the people who most influenced the life of the subject? How important were these people in the development of the subject's character? Were they positive or negative influences? How are they introduced and developed as characters? What differences are there between a fictional development of character and this nonfictional work? How would life for the subject have been different if these influences had not been present? Write about influential people in your life, asking yourself the same sorts of questions.

3. *Setting:* In fiction, the author can create settings appropriate to the story, inserting symbolic details and archetypes at will. The author of a biography or autobiography has little choice in the matter of surroundings. How much did those surroundings affect the subject's perception of life and the development of character? Include family setting as well as the physical surroundings. How would another setting have made things different? How do your surroundings affect your life? Write an episode in your own or another's life in which the real-life setting played a large part.

4. *Theme:* Traditional themes in autobiography and biography are the search for identity and triumph over obstacles. Look for evidence of these and other central ideas in the text. As a beginning, compare titles of various works suggested in the anthologies in the Bibliography. Does the title attempt to make a statement, as in *Up From Slavery,* by Booker T. Washington? Or is it more obscure, as in *I Know Why the Caged Bird Sings*? Make up titles for real or imaginary autobiographies and biographies of famous persons.

What would be the title of your own autobiography? Of the biography of your best friend?

5. *Style:* Older biographies are often adulatory toward their subjects. Older autobiographies are often pompous in tone. Look for evidence in the text regarding tone and attitude (see also "Persona and Persuasion: A Rhetorical Approach").

If the subject of a biography is a writer, examine the works written by that person. Seeing all written work as self-revealing allows us to compare the persona in those written works (see "Persona and Persuasion" for more on persona) with the representation given in the biography. Essays and speeches are especially useful since they can be read in a single class period.

Compare a biography with an autobiography, journal, and/or letters by the subject of that biography. Does the subject see himself or herself in a way different from the way others do?

See "From the Inside Out: A Linguistic Approach" for more specific examples of stylistic analysis.

Classroom Applications of "Biography as Art: A Formal Approach"

1. Read the rest of Sandburg's biography of Lincoln and write a book review or give an oral report to the class.

2. Compare the edited version of *Abe Lincoln Grows Up* with the original material in Sandburg's *The Prairie Years*. What has been omitted in the version for younger readers? In what other ways do the works differ?

3. Make a list of the major characters in *Abe Lincoln Grows Up*. How is each character introduced? How important were these people to Abraham Lincoln? How influential were they in the development of his character? Use the insights from this discussion to generate autobiographical writing about influential persons in your own life.

4. Once the book has been read and several aspects of its form have been covered, discuss how well the story has been written. (Note to the teacher: Remind students that they are entitled to have strong opinions, but that it is critically important for them to support their views with specific reference to the text and to the guidelines for using the formal approach.)

5. Write a critical review based on your opinions of *Abe Lincoln Grows Up*, supported by a formal analysis of the text. Bring in

reviews of the work from, for example, the *Book Review Digest.* (Note to the teacher: As students compare their reviews to professional criticism, point out examples from the student writing that compare favorably.)

6. Find several other biographies of Lincoln. Use the prereading book analysis in section 2 to compare the treatments of the subject by the various authors.

7. Read another biography of Lincoln. Compare it with *Abe Lincoln Grows Up.* Use the guidelines for using the formal approach for suggestions.

8. What would be an alternative title for *Abe Lincoln Grows Up?* Justify your reasons for choosing it.

9. Read anecdotes told and speeches written by Abraham Lincoln. Does the persona revealed in those writings match your image of Lincoln as portrayed by Sandburg?

10. Compare a fictionalized biography of Lincoln with *Abe Lincoln Grows Up.* What differences are there?

Inner Views:
A Psychological Approach

Jo McGinnis

> If growing up is painful for the Southern Black girl, being aware of her displacement is the rust on the razor that threatens the throat.
>
> —*I Know Why the Caged Bird Sings*

There is a familiar TV cartoon character who, in moments of conflict, is challenged by two opposing images that appear simultaneously on the screen. Over one shoulder an angel appears, giving advice about the right thing to do; over the other shoulder, a devil gives the wicked—but more appealing—advice. This comic image illustrates the tensions of deciding between what we *should* do and what we would *like* to do. When we recognize the interplay between the "should" and "would like to," we enter the realm of psychological ideas, and an exploration of these ideas can offer new possibilities for the analysis of literature. While a psychological approach to literature is far more complex than the angel-devil dilemma we see in the cartoon, it can give students a fascinating means of penetrating the often conflicting motives behind our own actions and the actions of people we are reading about in biographies and autobiographies.

It is Freud who has most influenced the thinking and the terminology associated with the psychological approach to literature, and his model of the human psyche—the Ego, the Superego, and the Id—can provide students with some basic knowledge of our psychological makeup. An elementary model casts our cartoon character as the Ego; the angel and the devil are replaced by the complex inner voices of the Superego and the Id, but devoid of the overtones of good and evil. A stable Ego, according to Freud, balances the dictates of the Superego with the desires of the Id. The Superego and the Id continually battle each other and perpetually besiege the Ego. Most of this badgering takes place in our unconscious, that area of our minds we might liken to closed, cluttered closets.

The Superego is a closetful of rules collected and stored from the moment of birth; it is a set of morals that the Ego lives by. Not only does the Superego try to direct the Ego's performance, but it also can punish the Ego with guilt for violations of these rules. Of course, the rules of the Superego differ with each of us. They may be positive, such as "you should brush your teeth," or they may be negative, as in "you should not throw stones." Imperatives like these usually originate with our parents and are augmented by the larger society, including church, school, law, the books we read, the movies we watch, and all else we observe about us. No matter what the source is, however, this collection of Superego regulations is as individual as a wardrobe.

The Id is a closetful of basic human needs and desires. Another way of looking at it is that like a naked, hungry baby, the Id wants and demands without consideration of others. It is often exemplified by various forms of self-indulgence, ranging from simple overeating to violent crime. The positive human needs of love and companionship come from the Id, yet the Id also incites negative actions if the Superego is not developed enough to counteract its power.

The Ego, then, is what we know of as the conscious mind, where reason and circumspection stabilize the precarious balance between the forces of the Superego and the Id. But the balance is still delicate: if the scales tip in favor of the Superego, the perfectionist in us causes us to react with guilt at any infraction of the rules; if the balance tips toward the Id, the "animal" in us emerges, tempting us to react with abandon. Often we are caught in some imbalance, overwhelmed by a sudden tipping of the scales, but we are always challenged by the need to restore equilibrium.

This challenge is a dominant theme in Maya Angelou's *I Know Why the Caged Bird Sings.* Not only does Angelou show us ways that she, as a southern black woman, has found to maintain this equilibrium, but she also describes ways that blacks in general have found to defend themselves against an often hostile white society. Anger erupts periodically throughout *Caged Bird,* each time threatening to tip the scales of balance in the Ego. When the cauldron of her emotions boils over, Angelou admits that the imbalance brings on paranoia, an irrational distrust based on the need to defend the Ego. Early in the narrative she writes, "In later years I was to confront the stereotyped picture of gay song-singing cotton pickers with such inordinate rage that I was told even by fellow Blacks that my paranoia was embarrassing" (7). This paranoia, she says, may be traced to a single incident in her life: Momma's confrontation with the "po-whitetrash" at the store in Stamps (22–27).

The stage for this drama is carefully set: Angelou explains first the rules of the black community, rules based upon cleanliness and respect for one's elders. She writes, "Everyone I knew respected these customary laws, except for the powhitetrash children." One summer morning, Maya is raking the dirt yard into a pattern of half-moons, symbolic of the order and neatness in their lives. Momma, the embodiment of the Superego, comes out to approve her work. In Momma we see the forces of the church, school, and parents; even her starched white apron is a visual representation of the Superego.

Then the powhitetrash girls appear over the hill, headed toward the store. The details of their appearance—dirty cotton dresses and greasy, uncombed hair—contrast sharply with the orderliness of Momma's world. Their outward appearance is matched by their behavior. Their mocking disrespect for Momma agitates Maya. Her balance wavers: "The world had taken a deep breath and was having doubts about continuing to revolve." The scales tip violently when one of the girls stands on her hands in front of Momma: "Her dress fell down around her shoulders, and she had on no drawers. The slick pubic hair made a brown triangle where her legs came together." Maya fumes and attempts to control her rage, imagining in detail what she would *like* to do: "I thought about the rifle behind the door. . . . I wanted to throw a handful of black pepper in their faces, to throw lye on them, to scream that they were dirty, scummy peckerwoods." But her Superego is continually monitoring her behavior, controlling her impulses toward those who have tried to diminish Momma's power. Momma's presence, that symbol of the Superego, restrains her actions.

Sent inside by Momma, Maya knows that she is "as clearly imprisoned behind the scene as the actors outside were confined to their roles." She wants to beg Momma: "Come on inside with me. If they come in the Store, you go to the bedroom and let me wait on them. They only frighten me if you're around. Alone I know how to handle them." However, Momma, who knows the ways of the white people, takes pride in maintaining control over her emotions and takes comfort from her faith. She continues to stand with calm dignity and to hum her hymns. Finally the girls go away, and Angelou writes: "Whatever the contest had been out front, I knew Momma had won." Balance is restored, and Maya rakes the yard into a new design.

This scene raises many questions for discussion in class. Why is Maya frightened only if Momma is around? How would Maya have handled the powhitetrash if Momma had not been present? Would she have given in to the desires of her Id, or would her Superego have been able to restrain her from excess violence? Eventually Maya will have to decide, as we all do, how to handle the tension of decision making in stressful situations. Will she handle it like Momma, whose Superego defers gratification of the Id? Or will she behave like Mother Dear, who believes in immediate gratification? Or Father Bailey, who abides by the Superego's rules outwardly, but occasionally slips across the border?

Choices like these remain a personal challenge to all of us. We may wish for the simplicity of the two clear choices of action offered to our cartoon character. Or we may wish that we could avoid choice by having someone tell us what to do. In reality, there are often many options to choose from, and none of them very clear. We listen to many voices giving us conflicting advice. The choices we make, like those depicted in literature, depend on a precarious and individual balance. The psychological approach to literature provides insight into character development, our own as well as others', by trying to identify and to understand the forces that motivate us all.

Guidelines for Using the Psychological Approach

1. Select a scene from the text in which one of the characters must decide what to do and in which there is a conflict about what ought to be done.
2. Ask students to identify that conflict in terms of a balance between the forces of the Superego (what the conscience demands or what society expects) and the forces of the Id (what would be most pleasurable or easiest).
3. Working as a class or individually, list all the options available to the character in this conflict. Which options are influenced by the Superego and which by the Id?
4. Identify any significant object, image, or sensory stimulus that might symbolize the force of the Id or Superego.
5. Construct an imaginary dialogue in which the Superego and the Id try to influence the decision of the Ego in balancing conflicting demands.
6. Identify the climactic moment of the scene in which a decision is made or no action or decision is taken at all.
7. Describe the consequences of the action.

Classroom Applications of "Inner Views: A Psychological Approach"

A Situation from I Know Why the Caged Bird Sings *for Psychological Analysis: The "Hot" Church Service (32-37):*

The conflict: Maya fears the loss of control over her composure when Sister Monroe threatens to repeat her emotional outburst during the church service and to attack Reverend Thomas. "If I lost control, two things were certain to happen. I would surely pee, and just as surely get a whipping."

The force of the Id: The Id wants her to laugh at something funny. The Reverend Thomas is someone detestable, because he eats so much and makes the food get cold when he says his long prayers before meals. Bailey is the symbol of the Id, nudging her and whispering, "I say, preach it," knowing it will make her laugh.

The force of the Superego: The Superego tells Maya that laughing in church is wrong. It would show a lack of respect for her elders, and "children should be seen and not heard." Momma is the symbol of the Superego. Angelou writes: "I looked toward Momma . . . hoping that a look from her would root me safely to my sanity." Later, when Maya is desperate to control herself, she tries to use her own means of keeping a lid on her impulses: "If he [Reverend Thomas] appeared just a little sad or embarrassed, I could feel sorry for him. . . . My sympathy for him would keep me from laughing."

The tipping of the scales: Reverend Thomas's false teeth pop out of his mouth when Sister Monroe hits him on the back of his head with her purse. They lie at her feet, and Bailey says, "I'd like to see him eat dinner now." Maya struggles desperately to restore balance, but succumbs when Reverend Thomas picks up his teeth and gums, "Naked I came into the world, and naked I shall go out."

The consequences: The forces of the Id are irresistible. "I didn't try any longer to hold back the laugh . . . I didn't know there was that much in the whole world. It pressed at all my body openings, forcing everything in its path." Uncle Willie gives them both a whipping.

Other Questions to Examine from a Psychological Perspective:

1. "Laughter so easily turns to hysteria for imaginative children" (37). Define *hysteria* and *imaginative*. Explain what Angelou means by this statement, relating it to the incident in the book. Relate it to something in your own experience that might support the statement.

2. "In later years I was to confront the stereotyped picture of gay song-singing cotton pickers with such inordinate rage that I was told even by fellow Blacks that my paranoia was embarrassing" (7). "I suppose my lifelong paranoia was born in those molasses-slow minutes" (24).

Define *paranoia*. How would you explain the term to someone, using Maya Angelou's experiences to illustrate the meaning of the term?

3. "I hated and dreaded the long winter nights when late customers came to the Store to sit around the heater roasting peanuts and trying to best each other in telling lurid tales of ghosts and hants, banshees and juju, voodoo and other anti-life stories" (133).

   What does Angelou mean by calling these stories "anti-life"? (You may want to look up the words first in an unabridged dictionary.) What is it about them that caused her fear and dread?

4. "It was a rare compliment in a world of very few such words of praise, so it balanced being touched by [Mrs. Taylor's] dry fingers" (134).

   Explain what emotions Maya was experiencing at this moment, relating them to the concepts of Id and Superego. What does Maya mean by "balanced" in this passage?

5. When Maya receives a valentine from Tommie Valdon, she feels afraid: "My questions fell over themselves, an army in retreat. Haste, dig for cover. Protect your flanks. Don't let the enemy close the gap between you" (121–22).

   What voices of the mind are these, the Superego or the Id? Justify your opinion by explaining why the voices would be pressuring Maya in this situation.

6. "Maybe . . . because children have a built-in survival apparatus, I feared he [Brother Taylor] was interested in marrying Momma and moving in with us" (129–30).

   What does Angelou mean by a "built-in survival apparatus"? Is there evidence in other parts of the book that such an apparatus is at work in Maya? Explain how it works in those instances.

7. "Momma [was] always self-conscious at public displays of emotions not traceable to a religious source" (131).

   Explain this statement from what you know about Momma after reading the book. What would the voices of Momma's Superego say to her whenever she saw someone displaying emotion "inappropriately"?

8. We all have models that we try to pattern ourselves after, and those models become a part of our Superego. What characteristics about Mrs. Flowers do you think became part of Maya's Superego?

9.   "Of all the needs (there are none imaginary) a lonely child has, the
     one that must be satisfied, if there is going to be hope and a hope
     of wholeness, is the unshaking need for an unshakable God" (19).
     Explain Angelou's statement in your own words, considering
     especially what she means by a "hope of wholeness." Relate the
     statement to what you know about Maya as a child and what her
     needs were. What do you suppose filled that need in Bailey?

10. What strategies did Maya use in order to avoid conflict or getting
     into trouble in her childhood years? Use specific behaviors and her
     reasoning behind them, considering especially her behavior in
     church, her walk to the white part of town, and her behavior in
     the store.

11. To be proud and sensitive was a "double-tiered barrier" in the
     path of Uncle Willie, in Angelou's opinion. Explain this statement
     and examine it in relation to the lives of other characters in the
     book (e.g., Momma, Maya, Bailey, Mother Dear). Does evidence
     exist in the book that others faced such a barrier?

12. Angelou describes the tent meeting on pp. 102–11. As the church-
     goers walk home, they pass by the honky-tonk. Angelou writes:
     "The people inside had forsaken their own distress for a little
     while." Compare and contrast the churchgoers with the people
     inside the honky-tonk, especially considering what we know about
     the Superego and the Id.

13. How does the Angel of the candy counter (156) fit in with your
     understanding of the psychological forces of Superego and Id?

14. Imagine the consequences if Maya had chosen not to take action
     when she did, as, for example, when she drives the car down the
     hill and back across the border from Mexico; or when she per-
     sistently applies to become a streetcar attendant; or when her
     father's girlfriend calls her mother a whore. Analyze these scenes
     in terms of balancing the Ego between the forces of the Superego
     and the Id.

15. Imagine, as Maya does when she pictures Momma going to the
     white dentist in town and settling the score with him in such a
     satisfying way, an ending to any of the scenes in the book in which
     Maya feels angry or hurt. Construct a satisfying ending to the
     scene.

16. Draw upon personal experience to analyze a situation in which
     you or someone you know struggled to maintain composure in a

time of conflict. (It may be as simple as the urge to go off a diet.) Fictionalize the account, if you wish, and tell it in the form of a story, including an inner dialogue between at least two conflicting voices. Build the story to a climax in which the character either succumbs to one of the demands or compromises. You may use one of the scenes from the text as a model.

Then and Now:
A Historical Approach

Nora Bellmann, Sandra Johnson Treharne, and
Lindley Hunter Silverman

We are here, we arrived, our roots are in the earth of these years.

—*Abe Lincoln Grows Up*

Readers of biography have high expectations. We look for subjects to come alive on paper and leap off the page. We read with an eye for gesture, an ear to idiom. We watch for twinkling eyes and raised eyebrows. Although we expect the biographer to breathe new life into the subject, that alone is not enough. We demand more.

We expect biographers to satisfy our interests not only in the life but also in the times of the subject. We are eager to plunge into other eras, to experience the colors, shapes, smells, and textures that influence the subject. We beg for details of flavors and fashions, the particulars of people and places.

We expect a great deal, and in Carl Sandburg's *Abe Lincoln Grows Up* our expectations are met. While skillfully illuminating Lincoln's childhood and youth, Sandburg also animates one of the most vital periods in American history—the opening of the western frontier. This successful integration of Abe's personal history into the context of our broader national history makes *Abe Lincoln Grows Up* a perfect target for an analysis using the historical approach to biography. This approach has long been a favorite because it focuses on supplementary information that reveals the halo of history surrounding every biographical subject. *Abe Lincoln Grows Up* provides a firm foundation in United States history between 1776 and 1831; national as well as local events are interwoven throughout the biography.

The scaffolding for the historical approach is dates and places. Both are easily recognized by readers, and they signal chronological and geographical progress in *Abe Lincoln Grows Up*. Sandburg punctuates the text with dates usually connected with special events; for example, the biography begins in 1776 with the Declaration of Independence. In 1802, the Lewis and Clark Expedition successfully traverses the Northwest Territory. Abe is born on February 12, 1809. In 1817, Abe's mother, Nancy Hanks, dies of the "milk sick" (undulant fever); two years later his father, Tom Lincoln, remarries, and Sarah Bush becomes Abe's stepmother. Robert Owen establishes the utopian community of New Harmony, Indiana, in 1825. The book closes in 1831, when Abe leaves home in Goose Nest Prairie, Illinois, to seek his fortune in New Salem.

Dates usually have places associated with them, and this narrative is peppered with geographical references. Sandburg takes us through the Cumberland Gap, down the Wilderness Road, through the still-untamed lands of Kentucky and Indiana, into the small towns of Mill Creek and Hodgenville, Little Pigeon Creek and Decatur. We cross the Ohio River, float down the Mississippi, ford the Sangamon. By following Abe's and his ancestors' footsteps we vicariously confront the virgin wilderness of the expanding frontier and the powerful influence it had on the early pioneers.

Abe's roots dig deep in American soil. Seeds of the Lincoln family history were sown by Abe's grandfather, for whom he was named, a former captain in the Virginia militia and a farmer in the Shenandoah Valley; Sandburg includes his signature in the text. Amos Lincoln represented the family at the Boston Tea Party; Great-Uncle Jacob fought with Washington at Yorktown. Abe's maternal grandmother, Lucy Hanks, traveled the Wilderness Road from Virginia to Kentucky without a husband, carrying the baby Nancy in her arms.

These fragments of ancestral history illustrate the prevalent spirit of the times, a mood both restless and reckless. People poured west for many reasons: some were "hungry for new land, a new home"; others felt led by the Lord to tame the wilderness; half a million British convicts were pardoned for their crimes for moving to the frontier. A pot of gold beckoned from beyond the Rocky Mountains; to move west was America's Manifest Destiny. Yet fearsome dangers threatened the settlers: Shawnee, Miami, and Seneca tribes fought brutally among themselves and against the white men, and Indian scalps brought two dollars apiece to those who killed before being killed. "It was still a country . . . where wolves and bear, wild animals and the Indians still claimed their rights and titles, with tooth and fang, claw and club and knife" (15). Sickness lurked, and home remedies could not control epidemics. Harsh weather was a constant killer of crops, livestock, and people.

For all the difficulties Sandburg portrays, he also underlines the democratic spirit of the times: this era was the time of the people. American presidents of the period—Adams, Jefferson, and Madison—embodied in their leadership the ideals of the Revolution. Jefferson assured further vigorous expansion when in 1803 he purchased the Louisiana Territory from Napoleon for the unprecedented sum of fifteen million dollars. Kentucky had been admitted to the Union in 1792; statehood then followed for Tennessee (1796), Ohio (1803), Indiana (1816), and Illinois (1818). New inventions opened possibilities for industry and commerce: Fulton's steamboat, the *Clermont,* smoked its way from New York City to Albany in 1807. The 1816 census reported eight million inhabitants of the United States. The American Dream had been born.

How this dream was realized by or denied to the early settlers is demonstrated by Sandburg's copious details of frontier life. Attempting to show the external characteristics of the area where Abe Lincoln grew up, Sandburg tantalizes us with tidbits of research, aptly scattered throughout his biography. He captures the rhythm of frontier life by recording details of the language of the time, its pronunciation, spelling, syntax, and diction. Various living spaces are described: the 18' × 18' log cabin in which Abe was born and the "half-faced camp" they lived in that first year at Little Pigeon Creek, Indiana, are two such descriptions. A dozen eggs cost about five cents, but since money was scarce, barter was common. For example, in 1816, Tom Lincoln sold his Knob Creek farm for twenty dollars and four hundred gallons of whiskey. Most people grew their own food. Pioneer people were versatile: Abe worked a bull-tongue plow, butchered hogs, built his own raft, ferried goats across the river, and even peddled notions. Sandburg unearths ballads from Virginia that Abe's mother sang and an account of the customary picnic that accompanied public hangings. He even discovers the position for drunks in the stocks and the cost of the new Elizabethtown jail, built in 1797 for seven hundred dollars. These are some of the details of a time when buckskin was in vogue and the Bible was the only reading available. *Abe Lincoln Grows Up* is a biography historically rich in fact and statistic.

The biography is further shaped by the appearance of key figures of the period. Starting with Daniel Boone, whom Abe's grandfather Abe followed to Kentucky in 1782, Sandburg includes Henry Clay and Daniel Webster, spokesman for the "plain people." John James Audubon and Johnny Appleseed share an entire chapter, their individual stories contributing to the general pattern of "community human cross-weaves" that so captivated Abe. Sandburg's documentation of Abe's personal history also bears witness to the times; Abe's growth exemplifies the growth of the nation. We gain insights into important educational processes: how Abe learned to talk, write, think. No sophisticated pedagogy existed at the time. To attend the "blab school," Abe walked nine miles each way.

One facet of Abe's history draws special attention: his awareness of slavery and its development in America. Sandburg injects reminders of injustice that create a subtle undercurrent throughout the book. In 1816, half the population of Hardin County in Kentucky, where the Lincolns lived, was black and enslaved. In 1828, Abe sees "likely" slaves being sold at auction in New Orleans. The injustice of such practices is ultimately redressed later, beyond the scope of *Abe Lincoln Grows Up*.

The historical approach to biography emphasizes dates, places, factual events, the essential components of nonfiction. Threading this tapestry of time, terrain, and detail is the powerful idea of historical change. The years 1776–1831 represent one of America's most vigorous times of reaching and broadening; Sandburg documents "the lean times and fat." Land bought in Kentucky in 1782 cost forty cents an acre; in Indiana in 1816, an acre went for two dollars. Many of the first landowners, who "tomahawk claimed" their property by axing a mark into a tree, lost it in 1816 because they had "wrong papers"—or no papers—filed with the U.S. government. Prices changed, property changed, the landscape changed, the government changed.

And people changed. Abe Lincoln, whose cousin Dennis pronounced that Abe would "never come to much," stands tall and strong on the threshold of maturity at the end of the biography, his toughness the very product of the American frontier. "Peculiarsome Abe" eventually becomes one of America's most beloved and remarkable leaders.

Every biographer is to some degree a historian. Subjects never exist in vacuums, but within historical milieus with which they must constantly interact. This approach to biography facilitates our ability to view the life of the subject simultaneously with the period. Further, it allows us to contrast the past with the present. In this contrast we recognize not only how Abe Lincoln changes within the scope of history, but also how our view of history changes.

Guidelines for Using the Historical Approach

1. Identify by dates the scope of the biography. Relate the time period described to what was happening in the rest of the world at the same time: in other countries (especially if they happen to be mentioned in the text); in the United States; in your own state; in your own town; in your own family. What is included in or omitted from the work?

2. List the places mentioned in the work. Find all geographical locations on maps. One map should reflect what the area was like during the time the subject lived. Another map should be con-

temporary, to compare how the area has changed since. Different maps emphasize different information; try a topographical map, a climate map, a population-density map, a political map, etc.

3. What new inventions were introduced at the time portrayed in the work? What differences might those inventions have made in the lives of the people portrayed? Imagine what life must have been like without inventions that we take for granted now, for example, life in the desert Southwest without air conditioning and icemakers.

4. Research the clothing and the furniture styles of the period. Research all the categories listed in the chapter on the sociological approach.

5. Research famous people of the period. Who were the leaders of the country? Who were the popular authors, entertainers, influential people? How might these individuals have influenced the subject of the work?

6. Research the language of the period by listing words from the text that seem dated or peculiar and looking them up in a historical dictionary.

7. Look at newspapers and magazines from the period, especially at the advertisements and the popular stories of the day. What insights into the period do they give?

Classroom Applications of "Then and Now: A Historical Approach"

1. After reading the text, draw a map of the Lincoln family's migration west. Try to approximate direction and distance. Then compare your drawings with a contemporary map of the same geographical area. What does this tell you about Sandburg's accuracy in recreating the setting of the book? Salt relief maps may be constructed to further enhance understanding of the terrain and the breadth of the westward expansion.

2. Make a list of unfamiliar or unusual vocabulary words that were used in Abe's time. What are the histories of these words and why have some fallen into disuse while others are still used today?

3. Several books that Abe read are mentioned by title in the text. Read all or parts of them and select portions for discussion. Which ones probably influenced Abe, and how?

4. Research further those history-making personalities—General Washington, President Adams, John James Audubon—mentioned

in the text. How do others' impressions of them compare with Sandburg's?

5. Sandburg mentions Napoleon of France only briefly. Research and summarize what was going on in European history during the time of Lincoln's early life.

6. Select one historical event mentioned in the text and write a series of newspaper articles recording that event as it was happening. Actual newspaper clippings of the day might be obtained for comparison.

7. Present three different accounts of the same historical event (e.g., the opening of the American West), as recorded in various history books. How do they differ? In what ways are they alike? What aspects of the period are emphasized in each? How can you determine which account is "right"? It is always interesting to read a foreigner's interpretation of American history; try to find, for example, a British history of the United States as a comparison to standard American histories.

8. Read a standard history of the United States for this time period. List three historical points of this period that you feel Sandburg overlooked or skimmed. On what basis and for what purposes do you think Sandburg omitted or superficially presented these points? If they had been included, how might they have changed the historical point of view in the book?

9. Create a historical magazine to accompany the text. Advertisements and cartoons should be included along with articles that enlarge and embellish the world created by Sandburg in the text.

10. Research the breadth of material compiled on Lincoln and especially Sandburg's contribution. For example, how many books are available on Lincoln as listed in *Books in Print: Subject Index* or in the library's subject card catalog? Investigate how Sandburg went about his research on Lincoln, by reading portions of a Sandburg biography. How do other biographies of Lincoln differ from Sandburg's? Use the guidelines in "Judging a Book by Its Cover" to review other biographies for the report.

11. Write to the Lincoln Memorial in Hodgenville, Kentucky, 42748, requesting information on their museum. Locate other Lincoln memorials in various places in the United States through a library reference search.

12. You are Sarah Bush Lincoln. Write a letter to your stepson Abe.

13. You are Nancy Hanks Lincoln. Write a letter to your son, perhaps telling him of your hopes for his future.

14. Pretend you are Abe and have been asked to speak in front of the local social club on your impressions from your first visit to New Orleans. Prepare an outline for a fifteen-minute talk.

15. You are one of Abe's neighbors. Take him one of your problems and describe how he solved it.

16. You are a reporter for the Cumberland County Gazette. You have witnessed the fight between Dan Needham and Abe (chapter 26). Prepare a bulletin for the evening paper.

17. You are the middle son/daughter of a pioneer family. Write a journal entry for a day in June, 1820. Include details of what you had to eat, the kind of work you did, your relationships with members of the family, the weather, the natural setting around you, your encounters with neighbors and/or strangers, and social events.

18. Prepare a list of important dates and events that took place in Lincoln's lifetime (as shown here for teacher reference). Be prepared to explain what significance those events might have had in the life of Lincoln.

Important Dates and Events 1776-1865

1776 Declaration of Independence is signed.

1781 Americans defeat the British at Yorktown.

1789 George Washington becomes president of the United States of America. The Constitution is ratified and becomes the law of the land.

1790 Samuel Slater builds first water-powered cotton spinner. The black population of the U.S. is 750,000.

1792 Kentucky is admitted to the Union.

1793 Eli Whitney invents the cotton gin.

1796 Tennessee enters the Union.

1800 Washington, D.C., becomes the nation's capital.

1801 Thomas Jefferson is elected president.

1802 Lewis and Clark explore the Pacific Northwest.

1803 Louisiana Purchase doubles the size of the United States.

1808 Slave trade from Africa is forbidden by law (although trade within America continues).

1811 National Road to link the East with the Midwest is started.

1812 The United States and Britain fight the War of 1812.

1816 Indiana is admitted to the Union. United States population stands at 8,000,000.

1818 Illinois is admitted to the Union.

1820 Missouri Compromise ends the slavery dispute temporarily.

1823 The Monroe Doctrine warns Europe against interference in the affairs of the Western Hemisphere.

1825 John Quincy Adams is elected president. The Erie Canal opens. Thousands of slaves are transferred over the next fifteen years from the North (where industry is supplanting agriculture) to the southern Cotton Belt. New Harmony, Indiana, a utopian community, is founded by Robert Owen.

1829 Andrew Jackson is elected president of the United States.

1830 Three-fourths of the world's cotton is produced in the Gulf States. The demand for slave labor increases.

1861 Abraham Lincoln becomes president of the United States. The Civil War begins.

1863 The Emancipation Proclamation is signed.

1865 The Civil War ends. Abraham Lincoln is assassinated.

Important Dates and Events in Sandburg's Abe Lincoln Grows Up

1782 Abe Lincoln's grandfather Abraham moves from Virginia to settle in Green River, Kentucky.

1786 Abe's grandfather is shot by Indians; his son Tom, Abe's father, moves to Hardin County, Kentucky (Mill Creek).

1795 Grand "raisin' " of the Elizabethtown, Kentucky, jail is held.

1796 A slave named Jacob, worth $400, is hanged for killing his owner with an ax after being "reproved for sloth."

1806 Tom Lincoln marries Nancy Hanks on June 10 in Springfield, Kentucky.

1809 Abe Lincoln is born on February 12 in a cabin at Nolin's Creek, Kentucky (near Hodgenville).

1812 Lincoln family moves to Knob Creek, eight miles from Hodgenville.

1816 Abe's father sells the farm for $20 and four hundred gallons of whiskey, and the family moves to Little Pigeon Creek, Indiana.

1817 After surviving a winter in a pole tent, the Lincolns build a cabin.

1818 Abe's mother dies of milk sickness (undulant fever).

1819 Tom Lincoln remarries on December 2: Sarah Bush becomes Abe's stepmother.

1820 Indiana University opens. Abe is the wizard of the ax.

1822 Pigeon Creek Church is built. Tom Lincoln tithes twenty-four pounds of corn.

1823 Abe works as a farmer, specializing in butchering for 31¢ a day.

1825 Abe works as a boat carpenter, navigator, and ferryman.

1827 Abe is arrested for illegal transporting; warrant is dismissed.

1828 Abe is employed for $8 per month to float goods down the Mississippi River to New Orleans.

1830 Abe's family moves to Macon County, Illinois, after selling the Pigeon Creek Farm for $125. Abe peddles notions en route as the family moves to settle six miles south of Decatur, down the Sangamo (now Sangamon) River.

1831 The Lincolns move one hundred miles southeast to Goose Nest Prairie in Coles County, Illinois. Abe travels again down the Mississippi. Abe leaves home to seek his fortune in New Salem, Illinois.

Important Dates and Events 1929–1945

1929 The Stock Market crashes and the Great Depression begins. Herbert Hoover is elected president. Martin Luther King, Jr., is born. The population of America is 122,000,000.

1931 Scottsboro Trial begins for nine black youths framed on charges of rape. The boys are freed.

1933 Twentieth and Twenty-first amendments to the Constitution are ratified. FDR is elected president and the New Deal begins.

1934 Arthur Mitchell is elected the first black congressman.

1936 Jesse Owens wins four gold medals at the Olympics in Berlin as Hitler watches.

1937 Joe Louis wins heavyweight boxing championship.

1938 Crystal Fauset is elected the first black woman state legislator.

1939 World War II begins in Europe. Marian Anderson is denied the use of Constitution Hall in Philadelphia by the DAR.

1941 The United States enters WW II after the Japanese attack on Pearl Harbor, December 7. The Supreme Court rules separate facilities in railroad cars must be equal. FDR establishes Fair Employment Practices Commission to prohibit discrimination in defense industries. Adam Clayton Powell is elected the first black councilman in New York City.

1942 Anti-black riots in Detroit. The first black man is admitted to the Navy Reserves. The *Booker T. Washington* is launched by the Navy, captained by a black.

1943 George Washington Carver dies. The Congress for Racial Equality is organized. Race riots occur in Los Angeles, Detroit, Harlem, and Beaumont, Texas.

1944 The Supreme Court bans white primaries. The War Department abolishes segregation in the U.S. Army.

1945 FDR dies and Truman takes office as president. World War II ends as the U.S. drops an atomic bomb on Hiroshima. The United States becomes a charter member of the United Nations. Georgia repeals the poll tax.

Important Dates and Events in Angelou's I Know Why the Caged Bird Sings

*1928 Maya Angelou (Marguerite Johnson) is born April 4, in St. Louis, Missouri.

1931 Maya and her brother Bailey travel by train alone from Long Beach, California, to live with their father's mother, "Momma" Henderson, in Stamps, Arkansas.

1935 Maya and Bailey go to live with "Mother Dear" in St. Louis.

1936 Maya is raped by her mother's boyfriend, Mr. Freeman.

1937 Maya and Bailey return to live in Stamps.

1940 Maya graduates with honors from Lafayette County Training School and goes to live in Los Angeles with her father.

1941 Maya moves to San Francisco to live with her mother and Daddy Clidell. She attends George Washington High School.

1942 Maya attends the California Labor School.

1943 Maya spends the summer in Los Angeles with Daddy Bailey and, later, the junkyard kids.

1944 Maya becomes the first black trolley car conductor in San Francisco. She is graduated from Mission High School. Her son Guy is born.

*These dates are approximate, because Angelou gives only her age.

Ideals and Ideas:
A Moral/Philosophical Approach

Margaret Fleming

The needs of a society determine its ethics.

—*I Know Why the Caged Bird Sings*

Scene: A teachers' lounge in any school. Four teachers are having a lunchtime conversation.

Bunsen: *You're using a moral/philosophical approach to literature? Sounds dull to me.*

Tester: *To me it sounds dangerous—next thing you know you'll be accused of using literature to teach your own values.*

Artis: *The biggest danger I see is the risk of distorting literature in order to teach morality.*

Fillmor: *Wait a minute. I can understand the last two objections, but how does a moral/philosophical approach come off being dull?*

Bunsen: *Moral—ugh—reminds me of those self-righteous Victorians who put pantaloons on piano legs.*

Artis: *It reminds me of my old high school English teacher. She had us find a moral for every work of literature we studied: "The moral of* Hamlet *is 'Delay can lead to undesired results.' " It's a wonder I didn't end up hating literature forever.*

Tester: *Talk about distortion!*

Bunsen: *That's bad enough, but philosophy is worse.*

Fillmor: *How?*

Bunsen: *Oh, you know—it's so stuffy—and so hard to understand—all those big words and abstract concepts. How can you do that to your students?*

Fillmor: *Put your mind at rest. I don't teach philosophy as such. All I do with my students is try to discover the philosophical assumptions* that authors have—whether they believe that there is a divine plan for our lives, or that humans control their own destiny, or that events happen at random and without purpose. It makes a difference in understanding why characters make the moral choices they do.

Tester: *There's the risk I'm concerned about. When you talk about moral choices, you're teaching values.*

Fillmor: *I disagree. I'm teaching my students one way to analyze literature, helping them to infer the values held by literary characters and the reasons those characters have for holding them.*

Artis: *But aren't you ignoring the aesthetic experience of literature when you focus on morality?*

Fillmor: *I don't think so. In the first place, this approach is not the only one I use. But even if it were, it seems to me that the moral dimension of literature is part of its aesthetic appeal.*

Artis: *How so?*

Fillmor: *Because if it's the art of the writer that engages readers, isn't part of that art the construction of believable situations in which differing values conflict? Readers are engaged by the subject of a person—like themselves—faced with making important choices.*

Artis: *But the art of the writer isn't in the subject matter of literature; it's in the language—the way words and sentences are arranged.*

Fillmor: *But language has semantic content as well as linguistic.*

Bunsen: *Linguistic—ugh—that sounds as bad as philosophy. Reminds me of my old grammar teacher, Mister —*

Tester: *I have to admit that what you're saying has some validity—but I wouldn't touch it with a ten-foot pole. I give objective tests to make sure students have read the literature; I figure they can make moral judgments on their own.*

Artis: *Now that's what I call dull.*

Fillmor: *You have a point. Discussing moral choices is risky, but I believe the risk is worth taking in order to lead students to higher levels of thinking.*

Tester: *Yes, but let's be practical. How do you cover yourself if parents start making some of the objections I've raised?*

Fillmor: *Well, one way I've found successful is to use Kohlberg's model as a systematic method of examining moral choices.*

Artis: *I remember his name, but that's about all.*

Bunsen: *Yeah, so do I. That summer course I took three years ago—the professor went on and on about him, but I tuned out most of it because it didn't have anything to do with science.*

Tester: *Well, I've never heard of him at all. Could you explain his model to us—say in the next five minutes or so?*

Fillmor: *Well, this is a gross oversimplification, but here's how it goes: Kohlberg divides moral development into three levels. Each of them has two stages within it, but I won't go into that now. The first level is called* Pre-conventional. *Here one's moral choices are made on the basis of expected punishment or reward, or on the idea of exchange.*

Bunsen: *Like "I scratch your back; you scratch mine"—that sort of thing?*

Fillmor: *Exactly. Or it can be negative. "You hit me; I'll hit you."*

Tester: *Clear enough. What's the next level?*

Fillmor: *The second level is called* Conventional. *Here moral choices are made on the basis of obedience to authority or following a set of rules or laws.*

Artis: *I imagine that's the level at which most members of society operate.*

Bunsen: *You're an optimist.*

Fillmor: *The third level Kohlberg calls* Post-conventional. *Here the choices are made on the basis of principle, going beyond implicit obedience to a realization that the good of a society depends on the mutual cooperation of its members. The U.S. Constitution is an example of this level in that it embodies the ideals our country has agreed to live by.*

Artis: *What about the Golden Rule?*

Fillmor: *Yes, that's another good example.*

Tester: *The objective, I suppose, is to move students from the lowest to the highest level.*

Fillmor: *Ideally it is, but remember we're talking about characters in literature, not students themselves. If the students, by analyzing characters' motives, can progress to the point where they begin to analyze their own, why, so much the better.*

Tester: *You see, that's what I'm afraid of. I don't want to have parents accusing me of trying to change their children's values.*

Fillmor: *It's not a question of changing their values. All students have a right to their own beliefs, but I won't be caught in the trap of saying every value is as good as every other.*

Artis: *Of course not. For instance, could anyone claim that Hitler's values were as good as Schweitzer's?*

Bunsen: *Hitler could.*

Tester: *No, but if we say Schweitzer's were better, we're judging by our values, aren't we?*

Fillmor: *Right. I say it's impossible to teach without imposing our own values, at least some of the time. The school itself forces us to stress the values of punctuality and honesty, for example.*

Artis: *But those are values agreed upon by the community.*

Fillmor: *Exactly. And the reason for establishing them is probably Post-conventional—cooperation for the benefit of the society as a whole.*

Bunsen: *But a student could have the same value for a different reason—isn't that right?*

Fillmor: *Yes. A student could be punctual only out of fear of punishment. That would be Pre-conventional moral reasoning. Or the student could be punctual because of a belief that it is always good to obey rules. That would be Conventional. Post-conventional reasoning would realize that a school functions best when all its members agree to follow certain rules for their mutual benefit. If students straggle in late every day, learning—the business of the school—suffers.*

Tester: *That's interesting. I never thought about it quite that way before. Let's try another example. I want to be sure I understand. Take stealing. At a Pre-conventional level, a child will not steal "because Mommy will spank me if I do."*

Fillmor: *Right.*

Bunsen: *And at a Conventional level, the child will not steal because it's against the law.*

Tester: *Then at a Post-conventional level, the child will not steal out of respect for the rights of others.*

Artis: *That's all very clear, but what if the child should choose to steal?*

Fillmor: *The same levels would apply. The child might steal simply for the reward expected: "I like cookies, so I'll take that one."*

Bunsen: *Or because no punishment was in sight—no threat.*

Tester: *Yes, I see.*

Fillmor: *Or, also at the Pre-conventional level, the child might decide to steal as a sort of tit for tat: "You stole my cookie; I'll steal your peach."*

Tester: *But at the Conventional level—since choice involves respect for law or authority—the child would not be able to make the decision to steal.*

Bunsen: *Now, wait a minute. In certain segments of society, stealing is an accepted convention. A child would be following authority or the implicit "rules" of that society. Remember* Oliver Twist?

Artis: *That's frightening.*

Bunsen: *Maybe so, but you'd be naive to deny that it happens.*

Fillmor: *That's why it's important to progress to the Post-conventional level—so that we can be sure obedience to law or authority is consonant with principle and not just unthinking acceptance of what others around us do.*

Tester: *Can there be an example of stealing at the Post-conventional level?*

Artis: *I don't see how.*

Bunsen: *I do. Suppose you had a strong belief—based on principle—that ownership of private property is wrong. You would simply believe that everything belongs to everyone and help yourself to what you needed.*

Tester: *Then you wouldn't be stealing, according to your own lights.*

Artis: *But you would be, according to the owner of the property you took.*

Tester: *Wait. I've thought of a better example. Your neighbor has a pistol, and during an argument you hear him threatening to shoot his wife. You see him lay the pistol down on his picnic table, and when his back is turned, you slip over and steal it.*

Artis: *So your belief in the sanctity of human life takes precedence over your respect for private property.*

Bunsen: *That's it exactly.*

Fillmor: *And here's where we come back to literature. So often the moral choices characters make are not clear-cut. It's not just good versus evil. In fact, in literature, they are seldom that. Rather, they are choices between one value and another.*

Artis: *The greater of two goods.*

Bunsen: *Or the lesser of two evils.*

Fillmor: *I think that when we can discuss choices in those terms, we have distanced ourselves from individual values, either the students' or the teacher's. We can be objective in analyzing why characters take one course of action or another, or why one value predominates over another, also recognized as good. If, in the process, students come to see more clearly their own reasons for choices they make or the values they hold, well, that's a risk I'm prepared to take.*

Tester: *And you can defend that moral choice?*

Fillmor: *Definitely. I don't consider it my right to change students' values, but I do hope that they will be able to develop for themselves reasons for holding their values, reasons that are consistent with their intellectual development. I believe that's part of the responsibility of an educator. A teacher of literature is a teacher of moral consciousness.*

Bunsen: *Is that belief based on Post-conventional reasoning?*

Fillmor: *Absolutely.*

Artis: *I had a teacher once who said that all great literature is asking two fundamental questions:* What is the nature of reality? *and* How shall one live? *That's just what we've been talking about, isn't it?*

Fillmor: *Yes. The philosophical question and the moral one.*

Artis: *Perhaps the fusion of the two in artistic language is part of what constitutes the aesthetic experience. I'll have to think about that some more.*

Bunsen: *Well, folks, I hate to tell you, but it's time to go back to class. If we're late, we'll all be stuck with extra hall duty next week.*

Tester: *A clear example of Pre-conventional reasoning.*

Bunsen: *Right you are. I know my level.*

They all go off to class.

The foregoing discussion dramatizes the controversial nature of a moral/ philosophical approach to literature. Fillmor, however, has come some distance toward bringing the others around to accepting its validity and usefulness. Following Fillmor's lead, we will use Kohlberg's model of moral development—in a simplified form—to examine some of the major issues that present themselves throughout *I Know Why the Caged Bird Sings* and to consider the philosophical assumptions upon which moral decisions are based.

One expects from children a Pre-conventional level of moral development, and we see this level exemplified in many incidents of Maya's childhood. Her temptation to steal pineapple is weighed against "the possibility of the scent exposing me," and, she admits, she doesn't "have the nerve to attempt it" (12). It is clear that she is dissuaded almost entirely by fear of punishment. Using the same reasoning, she takes special care of Mrs. Flowers' book, unable to imagine the hideous punishment she would deserve for damaging such a prized possession. The corresponding reward principle operates when Maya admits to loving Bailey so much that she wants "to lead a Christian life just to show God I was grateful" (17). Maya here demonstrates a belief in God, but only a limited one. At this point she does not see herself as having any degree of control over her life.

An example of the exchange-of-favors stage of moral development is Maya and Bailey's pact not to tell on each other, no matter what happens. Its counterpart, the exchange of injuries, occurs when Maya deliberately breaks a dish prized by her employer, Mrs. Cullinan. Mrs. Cullinan has arrogantly persisted in calling Maya "out of her name," renaming her Mary for her own convenience. Maya's reasoning is clear: "You take no care of something I value, my name. I'll take no care of something you value, your dish." This is one of the few examples from her early life in which Maya makes a deliberate choice that she knows will influence events. She even violates the rules of her religious upbringing to do so. Obviously this is an important choice, one that prefigures her development into a woman capable of controlling her own life. It stands out in the context because Maya has, up to this point, had so little control of events.

An extreme example of this lack of control is the major trauma of Maya's youth, her rape at the age of eight by Mr. Freeman, who is living with her mother. Its ugliness is enhanced by the fact that even the adults involved with this experience seem to be operating at a Pre-conventional moral level. Mr. Freeman rapes Maya for personal gratification, like the child who steals a cookie, with no consideration at all for Maya or for her mother. He then tries to ensure Maya's silence by threatening to kill Bailey if she tells anyone (tit for tat). After Mr. Freeman is released, he is brutally kicked to death (the implication is that Maya's mean uncles are responsible), no doubt according to the Pre-conventional reasoning that a brutal crime deserves a brutal retaliation. Maya, the innocent victim of the rape, suffers for months, feeling that she must somehow have been guilty, must somehow have done something wrong, to provoke so much pain and hostility. Her feelings illustrate vividly the dangers of permitting children to remain at a Pre-conventional level. At a Conventional or Post-conventional level, she would of course still feel the hurt but would know she had done nothing against her beliefs and hence not feel so guilty. Unfortunately for Maya, the adult models around her at this time give her little help in moving forward in her moral development.

The persons in Maya's life whom she most respects do demonstrate Conventional or Post-conventional moral reasoning. They conform to societal codes of behavior, as well as to their own codes of fairness and generosity. Mrs. Flowers, a true gentlewoman, is for Maya "the measure of what a human being can be." Mrs. Flowers treats her like a human being, not just Momma's granddaughter or Bailey's sister. Miss Kirwin, the only teacher Maya remembers, treats all her students—rich or poor, white or black—with absolute impartiality. Her stepfather, Daddy Clidell, a self-made man, says without boasting, "If I'm living a little better now, it's because I treats everybody right" (186). These persons all base their conduct on genuine respect for others as fellow human beings.

By far the highest and best-developed example of Conventional moral reasoning in the autobiography is Momma. Momma brings up her grandchildren to be obedient, hardworking, studious, clean, and responsible. Her two commandments, as perceived by Maya in childhood, are " 'Thou shalt not be dirty' and 'Thou shalt not be impudent.' " When Mrs. Flowers compliments Momma on her fine sewing and says that she must be proud, Momma answers, "No, Ma'am. Pride is a sin. And 'cording to the Good Book, it goeth before a fall" (81). Momma's philosophy is theistic; she believes that God controls human life. Her authority comes from the Bible and her religion, and she practices what she preaches. "Her world [is] bordered on all sides with work, duty, religion, and 'her place' " (47). It might be argued that Momma's moral development is Post-conventional, at least at times, since she believes so strongly in the Golden Rule and "God is Love," and always acts according to her beliefs. Angelou tells us, "I don't think she ever knew that a deep-brooding love hung over everything she touched" (47). Is this authority or principle?

Momma represents one extreme within black society. But Maya comes to know others, one of whom is her own mother. Mother Dear is fair and honest. She never cheats; she has no need to do so. As Angelou explains it, "her beauty made her powerful, and her power made her unflinchingly honest" (174). Mother's code seems to respect not so much the rights of all individuals (which would be Post-conventional) as that which satisfies her sense of her own integrity. Maya has a similar personal code regarding lying: "It was understood that I didn't lie because I was too proud to be caught and forced to admit that I was capable of less than Olympian action" (242). Are Maya and her mother acting at a Conventional level because they are adhering to a personal rather than a universal moral standard? Or are they Post-conventional, representing a philosophical orientation that is existential in nature? Existentialists believe that humans have an obligation to construct a meaning for their own lives and to act in accordance with it. This seems to be what Maya is doing, since at this time in her life, she has moved away from Momma, and possibly from the theistic orientation Momma represents as well, to experience other lifestyles and other ideas.

One of the different lifestyles Maya experiences, with the values attendant upon it, is that of urban black society, which proves to be quite different from the small-town society of Stamps. "The needs of a society determine its ethics," says Angelou, describing the moral attitude prevalent in the black ghetto:

> . . . the hero is that man who is offered only the crumbs from his country's table but by ingenuity and courage is able to take for himself a Lucullan feast. Hence the janitor who lives in one room but sports a robin's-egg-blue Cadillac is not laughed at but admired, and the domestic who buys forty-dollar shoes is not criticized but is appreciated. We know that they have put to use their full mental and physical powers. Each single gain feeds into the gains of the body collective.
> Stories of law violations are weighed on a different set of scales in the Black mind than in the white. Petty crimes embarrass the community . . . (190).

This appears to be Conventional moral reasoning in its adherence to the unwritten rules of a society. It might even be considered Post-conventional or principled, since it goes beyond rules and conventions for their own sake to consider the welfare of the society as a whole, society in this case being the black community. Here the "grab" and "kick" orientation of Mr. Freeman and the uncles is subordinated to the principle of the greatest good for the greatest number, a cardinal principle of utilitarianism. This philosophy was better-known in the late nineteenth century, at least by name, than it is today, but we can see it operating here and influencing the moral choices of the black community.

The clearest example of Post-conventional moral development in the book, however, can be seen in the description of the junkyard community in Los Angeles where Maya lives for a month. In this microcosmic society, with its few, but stringent, rules, exists a true social contract, again based on utilitarian principle, consideration of the greatest good for the whole society. No two persons of opposite sex sleep together; everyone works; no stealing is allowed. The reasoning is that violations would bring in the police, and the community would be broken up. So far the moral level appears to be Conventional. But it goes beyond that. For Maya, the experience is a turning point in her life:

> Odd that the homeless children, the silt of war frenzy, could initiate me into the brotherhood of man. After hunting down unbroken bottles and selling them with a white girl from Missouri, a Mexican girl from Los Angeles and a Black girl from Oklahoma, I was never again to sense myself so solidly outside the pale of the human race. The lack of criticism evidenced by our ad hoc community influenced me, and set a tone of tolerance for my life. (216)

Since Angelou's autobiography deals with complex questions and with the values of interacting subcultures, it is difficult to pin down clearly the moral reasoning of individual characters and the implicit values behind the choices they make. Several incidents, however, provide examples of this kind of conflict.

The episode with the dentist is interesting because of the progressive downshifting of moral reasoning it involves. When Momma first takes Maya to the dentist, she appeals to him at a Post-conventional level, assuming that he will respond according to the Golden Rule. Her train of thought is something like this: "My grandbaby has a toothache; please treat her as you would wish to be treated." Dentist Lincoln (his name, if real, is ironic) responds, however, at a lower level: "My policy is I don't treat colored people" (160). This has the appearance at least of Conventional reasoning, with its emphasis on policy. Momma, being unsuccessful at the higher level, is forced to shift to a lower one; she reminds the dentist of a favor she had done him in the past by lending him money and asks him to return the favor now. The dentist continues to refuse and eventually is led to expose his Pre-conventional morality, a childish "I don't have to if I don't want to" orientation. His "policy" is revealed to be nothing more than personal distaste, expressed in terms of punishment: "I'd rather stick my hand in a dog's mouth than a nigger's" (160).

This is merely one example of the overriding moral question that pervades the book, the question of justice for black people. Justice is denied every time whites refuse to consider blacks participating members of the human race. Uncle Willie has to hide in the potato bin when certain white men decide to lynch someone—anyone—black. Mrs. Cullinan assumes that Maya's name is unimportant; any name for a black person is as good as any other. The commencement speaker assumes that blacks can achieve excellence only in sports. Maya is refused employment as a trolley car conductor because she is black. Examples abound throughout the autobiography, as they do in life, many of them conditioned by a Pre-conventional way of thinking about such questions, perhaps based on the implicit belief that fate has decreed a subordinate "place" for blacks. At one point Bailey asks Uncle Willie what colored people had done to white people in the first place to make them hate blacks so much. Bailey's Pre-conventional reasoning is obvious, but Uncle Willie has no answer for him. Many whites respond at a Conventional level, acting according to the rules or policies of *their* society, not society as a whole. The commencement speaker who praises Jackie Robinson and Jesse Owens is a good example. Another might be the San Francisco trolley car company, which perhaps finally decides to hire Maya only because of the legal implications of its refusal. Maya has to be seen, not as a black, but as a United States citizen, entitled to full protection of the law. But this is still policy, not principle. Except for the junkyard kids, few persons respond at a Post-conventional level to what Angelou calls "the humorless puzzle of inequality and hate" (168).

Angelou provides no answer to the moral question, and her autobiography shows no real progress in answering it. The progress she exhibits is in her own ability to come to terms with life, the maturing of her own philosophy. The implicit question posed by her book seems to be "To what extent can humans control their own destiny?" or, more explicitly, "Can a southern black female take charge of her life and achieve a measure of control?"

At the beginning of her narrative, Maya's answer would have had to be negative. Chapter 1 begins with three- and four-year-old Maya and Bailey being sent to Stamps to their grandmother, labels around their wrists as if they were so much luggage. When their father appears suddenly five years later, they are taken to St. Louis. After Maya's rape, they are sent back to Stamps. Five more years go by, and they are sent to California. Momma would have called this the working out of God's will; Maya accepts it fatalistically: "If other children didn't move so much, it just went to show that our lives were fated to be different from everyone else's in the world" (57).

A similar sense of fatalism foreshadows the anticlimax of Maya's eighth-grade graduation day. Waking early in the morning, full of joyous anticipation, Maya admits the fears she had harbored: "Somewhere in my fatalism I had expected to die, accidentally, and never have the chance to walk up the stairs in the auditorium and gracefully receive my hard-earned diploma" (147). Later, as the family walks toward the school, she feels "a sense of ill-fated timing" (148). After the white commencement speaker's insensitive and tactless address has totally disheartened the black audience, Maya in her rage and frustration feels the clutch of fate on her life. "It was awful to be Negro and have no control over my life" (153). She senses the cruel irony in a classmate's recitation of "Invictus," especially its concluding lines, "I am the master of my fate, I am the captain of my soul" (154). Nevertheless the occasion is not altogether hopeless; the class valedictorian restores a measure of dignity and pride to the audience by leading them in the Negro national anthem. Maya realizes then that she is and will be a survivor.

The incident that puts Maya in control of her life for the first time occurs during her visit to Daddy Bailey in Los Angeles when she is fifteen. With his customary lack of consideration, Daddy takes Maya miles across the Mexican border to a nightclub, where he abandons her for the company of a woman and only much later reappears, too drunk to drive home. Maya knows that she must assume responsibility, and she does. Without ever having driven before, she grasps the wheel of Daddy's car, somehow gets it started, and clumsily, determinedly, steers it toward home, bucketing for miles along dark and mountainous roads to the U.S. border.

The automobile is a powerful metaphor for Maya's newfound realization that she can take charge of her life and control it, albeit with difficulty. In a further demonstration of independence, she lives for a month in an abandoned car in a Los Angeles junkyard. The metaphorical significance of this vehicle is its being stationary. Living in it, Maya is safe, and she is secure in the junkyard community, but she is not progressing in any direction. Returning to San Francisco, she begins looking for a job as a trolley car conductor, encouraged by Mother Dear, who says, "'Can't Do is like Don't Care.' Neither of them have a home." Angelou explains, "Translated, that meant there was nothing a person can't do, and there should be nothing a human being didn't care about" (225). Maya's job as conductor is at once a sign of her success and a metaphor for it. The vehicle moves, but she doesn't have to fight to keep it, unlike Daddy's car, on course. She controls her progress, but only within certain limits.

Maya's pregnancy follows hard upon this experience. In its balance between control and predetermination, it is like the trolley. But its significance is that it furthers Maya's realization of independence. The act of conception is deliberately initiated by her; the acceptance of its consequences brings her to an awareness that she can, to a great extent, control her destiny.

> For eons, it seemed, I had accepted my plight as the hapless, put-upon victim of fate and the Furies, but this time I had to face the fact that I had brought my new catastrophe upon myself. (241)

The pregnancy itself turns out to be not a catastrophe but another maturing experience. When her baby is born, Maya is happy in his perfection, proud that he is totally hers, and transformed by the experience. No longer dependent, she now has someone dependent on her.

Angelou sums up her growing awareness, as she enters adulthood, of what it means to be a black woman in American society.

> To be left alone on the tightrope of youthful unknowing is to experience the excruciating beauty of full freedom and the threat of eternal indecision. Few, if any, survive their teens. Most surrender to the vague but murderous pressure of adult conformity. It becomes easier to die and avoid conflicts than to maintain a constant battle with the superior forces of maturity. . . .
>
> The Black female is assaulted in her tender years by all those common forces of nature at the same time that she is caught in the tripartite crossfire of masculine prejudice, white illogical hate and Black lack of power.
>
> The fact that the adult American Negro female emerges a formidable character is often met with amazement, distaste, and even belligerence. It is seldom accepted as an inevitable outcome of the struggle won by survivors and deserves respect if not enthusiastic acceptance. (231)

I Know Why the Caged Bird Sings ends with Maya, like her grandmother and her mother—all in their different ways—having become a strong and mature woman, a "formidable character" in her own right. She has learned to control her destiny to the extent possible and to take responsibility for her choices. She too is a survivor.

Guidelines for Using the Moral/Philosophical Approach

1. What does the subject of the book believe about the way events happen? Does a Supreme Being guide people's lives? Are certain things fated to happen? Is the destiny of humans and the universe controlled by impersonal, scientific cause and effect? Can human beings control their own lives? Is life essentially meaningless? Which of these beliefs are held by other persons in the work? Find passages in which the beliefs of different persons are stated or in which clues to their beliefs are presented.

2. Find examples of actions people take that are directly based on their beliefs. How would they have acted differently if they had held some other belief? Rewrite a description of an incident in which the person takes a different course of action based on a different belief.

3. Look at the events chosen and emphasized by the author. Can you infer from these what the author's philosophical belief is?

4. Do the philosophical beliefs of the author or any of the persons in the work change over the course of time?

5. Is there anyone who appears to have no belief or to be uncertain or confused? How does this uncertainty affect that person's actions?

6. Choose a situation from the work in which a person has to make a choice. Try to decide which choices would be appropriate for each of the beliefs identified above. Then use Kohlberg's stages of moral development to analyze the possible choices. Are there possible choices at each level for each philosophical orientation?

7. After identifying a choice in terms of its moral and philosophical dimensions, try to identify it in terms of a conflict between the Id and the Superego (see "Inner Views: A Psychological Approach"). Do this for several choices. When is it morally right to obey the demands of the Id? The Superego? Are there other choices that lie somewhere in between?

8. For any of the situations identified above as involving a moral choice, try to determine which the *author* thinks is right. What clues are there as to the author's preference?

Classroom Applications of "Ideals and Ideas: A Moral/Philosophical Approach"

The following charts show reasons for choices of action based on Kohlberg's three levels of moral development. Some spaces are deliberately left blank, although students may be able to think of reasons that would fit. As the class discusses possible choices open to characters—and there may be more than two—students will undoubtedly find some more valid than others. When two values conflict, there will be differences of opinion as to which should be chosen, and this is as it should be, for students have different philosophical assumptions. Such discussions, we believe, contribute to students' moral consciousness-raising as it develops their ability to recognize the values implicit in any piece of literature.

1. Mrs. Cullinan humiliates Maya. Should Maya break her dish or not?

	Break the Dish	Don't Break the Dish
Pre-conventional	If you're mean to me, I'll be mean to you. If I break the dish, I won't have to work for her any more.	If I break it, Momma will punish me.
Conventional	It's OK to treat whites inconsiderately; everybody does it.	I'm a good girl, and good girls respect others' rights. Destroying the property of others is wrong.
Post-conventional		I wouldn't want anyone to destroy anything I valued; so I won't destroy her dish.

2. Mr. Freeman rapes Maya, but his lawyer gets him off. Should her relatives kill him?

	Kill Mr. Freeman	Don't Kill Mr. Freeman
Pre-conventional	You were brutal to a member of my family; I'll be brutal to you. I can get away with killing him.	Whoever kills him could be caught and executed.
Conventional		Thou shalt not kill. Killing is illegal.
Post-conventional	Justice is above the law; the law failed to provide justice; therefore I will be an executor of justice.	Human life is sacred. It is never right to kill anyone. "Vengeance is mine; I will repay," saith the Lord.

Construct similar charts and discuss the moral reasoning for choices contemplated or made by various characters in *I Know Why the Caged Bird Sings*. Some situations are suggested below.

1. Should Maya and Bailey's parents send them to Momma to raise after the parents' divorce?

2. Maya loses control in church. What reasons are there for punishing her or not punishing her?

3. What is the moral reasoning behind looking for any black man to lynch in retaliation for the alleged offenses of another?

4. Momma punishes Maya for saying "by the way." What is her reason? What other reasons might be given for her decision or the opposite one?

5. Bailey stays out late to see a Kay Francis film without telling Momma. Should she punish him or not? Why?

6. Should Maya tell Mother about being raped? What reasons are there for her different options?

7. What level of moral reasoning is Mr. Freeman's lawyer using when he implies that Maya was raped because she had been deliberately provocative?

8. What is Maya's reasoning when she agrees to play lookout for Bailey and Joyce when they play "Mother and Father" inside the tent? How else might she have responded, and why?

9. Mother Dear and Daddy Clidell apparently skirt the edges of unlawful activities. What reasons can be given for and against this?

10. Why should Maya tell or not tell her family she is pregnant?

11. Why does Maya keep her baby instead of giving him up for adoption? What reasons could be given for the opposite decision?

From the Inside Out:
A Linguistic Approach

Jo McGinnis

> . . . pages and pages filled with words spelled out like the words in
> the spelling-book he had in school. So many words—heavy words,
> mysterious words!
>
> —*Abe Lincoln Grows Up*

"I don't need to see the inside, Mrs. Henderson, I can tell . . ." says Mrs.
Flowers (81). Momma is urging her to examine the French seams around
the armholes of Maya's dress. Maya is humiliated because she is stuck
underneath the upturned garment. Mrs. Flowers is uncomfortable: surely
she can appreciate the work without having to turn it inside out.

Momma, however, knows that there is more to making a dress than its
general effect. She takes pride in her craftsmanship and wants to show
there are no raw edges or loose threads. A linguistic approach to literature
proposes a similar close examination of the craftsmanship of a writer.
Parts of speech, sentence construction, and other linguistic features
worked into the fabric of a story are studied to explore how they contribute to the finished work.

The linguistic approach extends the traditional notion of grammar as
a part of the study of English. Grammar is often taught as a separate
function of the language, with the assumption that such knowledge will
somehow be transferable to skills in reading and writing. Many studies,
however, have shown little correlation between the ability to recognize
parts of speech, for example, and writing. The linguistics-oriented teacher
of literature brings the study of language out of isolation and bridges the
divisions between instruction in literature, in language, and in composi-
tion. Interlacing these three areas of instruction provides a more compre-
hensive and unified approach to English. When the literature experience
generates enthusiasm, the teacher can capitalize on that enthusiasm to
create interest in exploring the language used by effective writers. Once
students discover the linguistic elements of successful writing, they are

freed to experiment with the language. Continuing experimentation leads to increasing control in their own writing.

A linguistic analysis of literature can be a formal and systematic process, as outlined in the Guidelines. In this process, a writing sample of at least two hundred words is dissected to expose its syntax, diction, and semantics. The preliminary work involves counting—of paragraphs, of sentences, and then of individual words. (Much of this initial work is now being done with computers.) The next step is to identify specific features selected for emphasis; they can range from parts of speech to figures of speech.

A linguistic approach to a work does not have to be this formal or this systematic, however. The Classroom Applications at the end of this chapter include a number of suggestions for ways to ease linguistics and grammar into the literature and writing curriculum without overwhelming the teacher or the students with talk about right-branching and left-branching elements and compound/complex sentence structures, or heavy doses of parts of speech. To begin with, students might comment on whether the work is easy to read or difficult. What makes it that way? Does the author use too many big words? Are the sentences too long? Or monotonous, lacking any variety or complexity? Does the prose read like that in another favorite story or novel? Why or why not?

The essential work of this approach, regardless of whether the analysis is formal or informal, is to make the leap from identification of linguistic elements to a critical analysis of how those elements function. Circling adjectives in a writing sample can teach far more than how to recognize an adjective: the strengths and weaknesses of different types of adjectives become apparent when they are exposed. Isolating verbs may explain why one writing sample crackles with action while another moves at a slower pace. Even the definite article gains significance once it is seen how *the* may be used by an author to establish an intimacy with readers from the very first word in a work. A close linguistic analysis of Sandburg's *Abe Lincoln Grows Up* focusing on a variety of linguistic features reveals the type of insights that might be gained.

Linguistic Analysis

In the opening sentence of his biography of Lincoln, Carl Sandburg, poet and historian, establishes himself as a storyteller, in the tradition of "Once upon a time . . ." In prose that must be read like poetry, Sandburg writes:

> In the year 1776, when the thirteen American colonies of England
> gave to the world that famous piece of paper known as the Declara-

> tion of Independence, there was a captain of Virginia militia living
> in Rockingham County, named Abraham Lincoln.

Sandburg creates a tone of intimacy with his readers by speaking of things as if he and the reader share a common bond. Compare the original with a revision that replaces *definite articles:*

> In 1776, when thirteen American colonies of England gave a world a
> famous piece of paper known as a Declaration of Independence,
> there was a captain . . .

Sandburg's original assumes that the reader knows the importance of *the* year 1776, *the* thirteen colonies, *that* famous piece of paper, and *the* Declaration of Independence. To remove the definite articles would place a greater distance between the storyteller and the reader.

Sandburg continues his tale in a measured way. He does not allow the pace to quicken in the next paragraphs, although he describes a time of "much fighting." One way that he controls the speed of the narrative is by manipulation of *sentence structure.* "Normal" sentences in English are generally S-V-O ("The dog ate my paper") or S-V-C ("The dog is my friend"). Most writers follow this pattern about 75 percent of the time, attaching modifiers to the ends of the sentence to expand the basic structure (right-branching elements). Sandburg's second sentence is an example of a greatly expanded, but "normal," sentence construction:

> He was a farmer with a 210-acre farm deeded to him by his father,
> John Lincoln, one of the many English, Scotch, Irish, German,
> Dutch settlers who were taking the green hills and slopes of the
> Shenandoah Valley and putting their plows to ground never touched
> with farming tools by the red men, the Indians, who had held it for
> thousands of years.

Sandburg doesn't follow the normal arrangement as often as do most writers, however; he often rearranges the components of his sentences. Over half of Sandburg's first twenty-six sentences open with something other than the subject or subject "cluster." Six of these "abnormal" sentences are inversions, in which the verb comes before the subject. The storyteller's staple "There was a . . ." is one kind, as in the opening sentence of the narrative. Other sentences are inverted for a specific effect, as in sentences 6 and 7, whose parallel structure gives the four compass directions special emphasis: "To the south and west were the red men. To the north and east were white men. . . ." Other sentences that do not follow the normal order begin with clauses or phrases that are not part of the subject cluster (left-branching elements). There is an adverb clause at the beginning of the first sentence, for example:

> In the year 1776, when the thirteen American colonies of England
> gave to the world that famous piece of paper known as the Declara-
> tion of Independence . . .

Another example is in the first independent clause of sentence 11, which,
like the first sentence, is not only an inversion but has an adverb clause at
the beginning: "Though they were fighting men, there was a strain of
Quaker blood running in them. . . ."

Sometimes Sandburg separates the basic components of his sentences
by inserting words and phrases between the subject and the verb or
between the verb and the object to heighten suspense and build to a
climax:

> And she and Tom Lincoln and the moaning Nancy Hanks welcomed
> into a world of battle and blood, of whispering dreams and wistful
> dust, a new child, a boy. (32)

Any time the normal flow of a sentence is interrupted, a reader is required
to read more slowly, and thus is given the opportunity to savor the poetic
language.

There are other ways Sandburg controls the pace of his story. The
strings of compound sentences and the repetition of the *conjunction* "and"
contribute to a calm and stately tone reminiscent of the King James Bible,
as does the slightly archaic diction:

> Now Abraham Lincoln had taken for a wife a woman named
> Bathsheba Herring. And she bore him three sons there amid the
> green hills and slopes of the Shenandoah Valley, and they were
> named Mordecai, Josiah, and Thomas. And she bore two daughters,
> named Mary and Nancy. (5)

The repetition of key words and phrases is a way in which Sandburg
controls not only the pace but reader response. For example, a close look
at the *adjectives* he repeats in describing the major characters can show
the power of those words to trigger associations. Sandburg's care in using
evaluative adjectives (e.g., *beautiful, kind, stupid*) as opposed to
descriptive adjectives (e.g., *tall, curly, red*) is appropriate to a historical
treatment of his subject. Yet as a poet intimate with the connotative power
of language he selects certain words that have multiple meanings. For
example, Sandburg describes Lincoln's father:

> He was a slow, careless man with quiet manners . . . (12)
>
> In his slow way of talking—he was a slow and a quiet man—Tom
> Lincoln told them . . . (32)

In light of Tom's attitude toward "book larnin' " and his opposition to his son's "eddication," there is ambiguity in the adjective "slow" to describe him.

The word "dark" is a word used several times in the characterization of Nancy Hanks, Lincoln's mother:

> Her dark skin, dark brown hair . . . (25)
>
> She was shrewd and dark and lonesome . . . (25)
>
> She was sad with sorrows like dark stars in blue mist . . . (26)

"Dark" might be called a descriptive adjective in the first sentence, but it takes on a more evaluative meaning in the other references. Sandburg freely associates Nancy Hanks with a mysterious sadness and lonesomeness that lend rich connotations to the word.

The repetition of linguistic elements is only one of many poetic devices in *Abe Lincoln Grows Up*. Students once sensitized to language will point out others, such as alliteration and simile. It is important to keep in mind, however, that the work of linguistic analysis goes beyond the identification of elements of language. The objective is to find answers to the question, "Why did Sandburg say it this way?"

For the teacher who wants to help students make the leap from identification exercises to critical analysis, the following resources may prove helpful: Jean Malmstrom and Janice Lee have specific suggestions in *Teaching English Linguistically*. Edward P. J. Corbett's *Classical Rhetoric for the Modern Student* is a valuable reference, as is Francis Christensen and Bonniejean Christensen's *Notes Toward a New Rhetoric*. Walker Gibson, in *Tough, Sweet, and Stuffy,* has developed a "Model T Style Machine" to help classify writing samples into categories according to the language used by different authors. He compares, for example, the stripped-down, spare style of a "tough" writer like Ernest Hemingway with the "stuffy" prose of government pamphlets, and with the "sweet" rhetoric of advertising copy. His chart is a valuable tool for making linguistic evaluations.

From Analysis to Writing

When it is time to transfer the insights gained from critical analysis to student writing, the question "Why did the writer say it *this* way?" becomes "Why am *I* saying it this way?" Writing assignments tailored to increase the chances of transfer of knowledge from reading to writing, from a critical analysis to an immediate application of new insights, are the ideal. No patterned writing exercise can substitute for writing assignments that call for original thought and development on the part of the student. Just as a scrimmage practice does not substitute for Saturday's game, and exercise at the barre does not have the same value as the ballet performance, structured modeling exercises cannot replace other in-class writing assignments. Nevertheless, there are ways to focus on specific writing techniques as prewriting exercises.

Sentence imitation is one example of the kind of writing exercise that combines the skills of reading, language study, and writing. A student may choose appealing sentences from a work and then attempt to shape a different idea to the form predetermined by the author. The sentence structure should follow the original as closely as possible: where Sandburg uses a prepositional phrase with two adjectives preceding the object, for example, the imitation should do the same. Certain functional words (such as the common expletive "there was . . .") will remain the same. Action verbs, nouns, and adjectives would be equivalent replacements. An imitation of the first sentence of *Abe Lincoln Grows Up* might read:

> In the year 1982, when the film studios of Hollywood introduced to the public that funny creature from outer space known as E.T., there was a student at Magee Junior High School living in Tucson, Arizona, named Elliot Weiner.

In some happy instances like this one, the exercise might be used as a heuristic device to suggest a narrative worthy of expansion. The primary objective, however, is to gain expertise in the manipulation of sentence elements. It is possible for students to imitate the functions of the parts of speech with only the innate knowledge possessed by the native speaker of the language. It isn't necessary to label each clause and part of speech except as it makes the work easier to talk about. Students may choose complexity of structure to suit their own voices, their own skills, and their own desire for challenge.

There are other disciplined exercises that teach reading and writing skills simultaneously. Using excerpts from literature in *dictation,* for example, is a European tradition that gives students practice in listening carefully and in exercising writing skills by writing model sentences. If the teacher introduces unfamiliar words before reading the material aloud, dictation practice becomes a study of vocabulary as well.

An idea borrowed from Benjamin Franklin is the exercise of taking notes on several paragraphs of writing in a kind of rough outline of ideas, and then rewriting the material based upon the notes. Franklin in his *Autobiography* describes how he used the *Spectator* as a model for writing, and he was pleased with his progress when at last his rewritten material compared favorably with the original.

Sentence-combining exercises involve breaking down embedded sentences into "kernel" sentences, each containing one element of information. Reconstructing those kernels into new longer sentences is a means of experimenting with subordination and the structure of complex sentences.

These suggested writing patterns are warm-up exercises for frequent and informal self-directed writing assignments. Not every writing assignment, of course, needs to be turned in for evaluation; students may share their ideas with the class by reading passages aloud to show how they adapted ideas and patterns to suit their own purposes. Just as they will watch carefully a new dance step to incorporate into their own routine, they must examine closely and then experiment with new and more effective techniques in writing.

The overriding rationale for using the linguistic approach to literature is that writing should never be far removed from reading, and that neither should be severed from an awareness of language. There is a continual challenge to the teacher of English in the paradox of explaining language with language, in using language to decipher the messages in the riddles of reading and writing. Teachers of English can use the linguistic approach to show why successful writing *is* successful—and at the same time give students tools with which to emulate it.

Guidelines for Using the Linguistic Approach

1. Count and classify the following:
   a. Total number of words
   b. Number of T-units (independent clauses)
   c. Number of dependent clauses
   d. Number of fragments
   e. Number of prepositional phrases
   *f. Number of nouns
   *g. Number of adjectives
   h. Number of articles
      (1) Definite
      (2) Indefinite
   *i. Number of finite verbs
      (1) Active
      (2) Passive
      (3) Copula
   *j. Number of verbals
   k. Number of coordinate conjunctions
   *l. Number of "left-branching" sentence modifiers (sentence openers preceding the subject)
   *m. Number of "right-branching" sentence modifiers

      *n. Compounded elements (words and structures)
      *o. Repetitions (words and structures)
      *p. Inversions
      q. Number of paragraphs

2. Express the following ratios as decimals:
    a. Words/T-units
    b. Dependent clauses/T-units
    c. Nouns/total words
    d. Adjectives/nouns
    e. Verbs/total words
    f. Verbals/finite verbs
    g. Coordinate conjunctions/total words
    h. Definite articles/total words

3. Look for examples of stylistic use of the language. Consider such schemes and tropes as similes, metaphors, alliteration, plays on words, double meanings, and assonance.

4. For the starred items in section 1, make lists on a separate page. Use these lists as the basis for generalizations and comparisons. Notice such things as whether the words are abstract or concrete, polysyllabic or monosyllabic, descriptive or evaluative. Other questions to consider: What features besides those above might be noted? What features does a linguistic analysis fail to take into account?

Classroom Applications of "From the Inside Out: A Linguistic Approach"

1. Type and reproduce an excerpt from *Abe Lincoln Grows Up,* as in the example that follows (from pp. 22–23), with no punctuation marks or paragraph divisions. Each student will have a copy to look at and to mark as the teacher reads the material aloud. If the story is an unfamiliar one, the teacher may give a brief "book talk" to introduce the situation. The students then listen to the teacher read the excerpt while following along on their copies, marking each minor pause or dip in the teacher's voice with a single slash and each "terminal" drop in tone with a double slash. The process may be repeated, this time a little more rapidly, for students to double-check their impressions. Then allow enough time for rewriting the material so that students may add all punctuation and paragraphing they think necessary (twenty to twenty-five minutes will be needed). Go over the work in class, discussing optional punctuation and the various rules and formal standards involved. Students may make

corrections on their own papers. (This activity works well on the overhead projector.)

> *Example:* On the morning of february 12 a sunday the granny woman was there at the cabin and she and tom lincoln and the moaning nancy hanks welcomed into a world of battle and blood of whispering dreams and wistful dust a new child a boy a little later that morning tom lincoln threw some extra wood on the fire and an extra bearskin over the mother went out of the cabin and walked two miles up the road to where the sparrows tom and betsy lived dennis hanks the nine year old boy adopted by the sparrows met tom at the door in his slow way of talking he was a slow and a quiet man tom lincoln told them nancys got a boy baby a half sheepish look was in his eyes as though maybe more babies were not wanted in kentucky just then the boy dennis hanks took to his feet down the road to the lincoln cabin there he saw nancy hanks on a bed of poles cleated to a corner of the cabin under warm bearskins she turned her dark head from looking at the baby to look at dennis and threw him a tired white smile from her mouth and gray eyes he stood by the bed his eyes wide open watching the even quiet breaths of this fresh soft red baby what you goin to name him nancy the boy asked abraham was the answer after his grandfather

2. In an exercise of sentence combining, divide the class into four groups. Give each group one of two short paragraphs from the text so that half the class is working on one paragraph and the other half of the class the other paragraph. If the class has had some experience with sentence combining, they will be familiar with the concept of breaking down embedded sentences into "kernels." Have the groups break down the sentences in the paragraph into as many kernels as they can find.

After an appropriate period of time, the groups exchange with the groups breaking down the other paragraph, so that now each group is working with a different paragraph than the one they disassembled. The new assignment is to rewrite the paragraph by reassembling the kernel sentences provided into a paragraph, using their best judgment as to how the elements should be combined. Since two groups will be working with the same paragraph, the two efforts may be compared with each other, as well as to the original paragraph written by Sandburg. Some students may prefer their own way of expressing the ideas to the way that Sandburg chose to write it. Ask questions that make the students hypothesize about the reasons Sandburg arranged the material in the way he did. Examples of paragraphs to use are as follows:

From p. 1 (note: to prevent confusion, inform the class that the Abraham Lincoln mentioned here is the grandfather of Abe Lincoln):

> The year was 1776.
> The colonies gave that piece of paper.
> The colonies were American.
> The colonies were of England.
> That piece of paper was for the world.
> That piece of paper was famous.
> That piece of paper was known as the Declaration of
>   Independence.
> There was a captain.
> The captain was of the militia.
> The militia was from Virginia.
> The captain was living in Rockingham County.
> The captain was named Abraham Lincoln.

From p. 32:

> It was morning.
> It was February 12.
> It was Sunday.
> The granny woman was there.
> The granny woman was at the cabin.
> The granny woman welcomed a child into the world.
> Tom Lincoln welcomed a child into the world.
> Nancy Hanks welcomed a child into the world.
> Nancy Hanks was moaning.
> The world was of battle.
> The world was of blood.
> The world was of dreams.
> The dreams were whispering.
> The world was of dust.
> The dust was wistful.
> The child was new.
> The child was a boy.

3. Select a passage from the text that contains a number of adjectives. Once the students have underlined all of the adjectives, discuss whether they are *evaluative* adjectives or *descriptive* adjectives. Experiment with replacing descriptive adjectives with evaluative adjectives. How does this change the effect of the passage?

4. Select a passage from the text that contains a number of specific, concrete nouns, as on p. 21: ". . . and at noon the men all crowded into the Haycraft double loghouse to eat hearty from loaves of bread baked in a clay oven, roast shotes, chickens, ducks, potatoes, roast beef with cabbage and beans, old-fashioned baked custard and pudding, pies, pickles, and 'fixin's.'" Compare it with other sen-

tences like the one on p. 26: "She believed in God, in the Bible, in mankind, in the past and future, in babies, people, animals, flowers, fishes, in foundations and roofs, in time and the eternities outside of time. . . ." Once the students have underlined all of the nouns and decided whether they are specific or general, abstract or concrete, experiment with replacing the specific, concrete nouns with more general, abstract ones. What effect does this have on the text?

5. Adverbs, like adjectives, are often *evaluative* rather than purely *descriptive*. They tend to add value judgments to writing by telling *how* something was done. After students have identified and perhaps figured a proportion of adverbs to the total number of words in a sample of Sandburg's writing, they may discuss how evaluative those adverbs are in the passage. Sprinkle some strongly evaluative adverbs and "empty" adverbs like *very, such,* and *so* into a paragraph by Sandburg to see the effect that adverbs have on writing. Students may discover that Sandburg uses few adverbs but that there are instances in which he uses them to effect, as in the following example:

> The country in Hardin County and around Elizabethtown was *still* wilderness, with *only* a few farms and settlements. Kentucky had been admitted to the Union of states . . . but it was *still* a country of uncut timber, land unknown to the plow, a region where wolves and bear, wild animals and the Indians *still* claimed their rights and titles, with tooth and fang, claw and club and knife. (15)

6. Teachers often point out repetition as something to beware of in student writing. Yet Sandburg often uses repetition for effect in *Abe Lincoln Grows Up.* Consider the sentences describing Nancy Hanks on p. 26 in which the beginnings are alike: "She was sad . . . She had seen . . . She had seen . . . She believed . . . She knew . . ." Whenever repetition like this occurs (a figure of speech called *anaphora*), we can be sure that the author has used it deliberately, as it is generally reserved for passages where the author wants to produce a strong emotional effect.

7. Another type of repetition used for effect is the addition of the conjunction *and* where it isn't needed or ordinarily found. What effect does this have in passages like the following paragraph from p. 5? "Now Abraham Lincoln had taken for a wife a woman named Bathsheba Herring. *And* she bore him three sons there amid the green hills and slopes of the Shenandoah Valley, *and* they were named Mordecai, Josiah, and Thomas. *And* she bore two daughters, named Mary and Nancy."

8. What is the effect of leaving out a conjunction where one is expected and of piling up items in a series? Consider the passages on p. 26, again describing Nancy Hanks: "She believed in God, in the Bible, in mankind, in the past and future, in babies, people, animals, flowers, fishes, in foundations and roofs, in time and the eternities outside of time. . . ." and "Everyday came scrubbing, washing, patching, fixing."

The Power of Myth:
An Archetypal Approach

Margaret Fleming

Days came when he sank deep in the stream of human life and felt himself kin of all that swam in it, whether the waters were crystal or mud.

—*Abe Lincoln Grows Up*

"What is it that goes on four legs in the morning, two legs at noon, and three legs in the evening?" "Man, who crawls in infancy, walks upright in the prime of adulthood, and uses a cane in old age." Oedipus' answer to the ancient riddle of the Sphinx, which links the cycle of a single day with the cycle of a human life, is a clear example of an archetype. Archetypes are enduring, universal symbols, which arise from what the psychologist Jung calls the "collective unconscious," that body of shared experiences not restricted by culture but common to all humankind: natural cycles, growth, family relationships, physical surroundings. As with other symbols, the concrete object or experience comes to stand for the abstraction associated with it; thus fire represents warmth, both physical and emotional; blood passion; gardens fertility; deserts sterility; and the wilderness an unknown terror. All these and many others appear and reappear with virtually the same significance in folklore and literature from cultures around the world. Although common, these archetypes are often well internalized; an effort may be required to bring them to conscious awareness. Once recognized, however, they may be seen everywhere—in fairy tales, in TV shows, in figures of speech, in color associations, in patterns of human experience.

Archetypes might also be called the deep structure of literature. Myth, folklore, history, poetry, drama, biography—all embody archetypes, using them for different didactic and artistic purposes and expressing them through a wide variety of surface features. *Oedipus Rex,* "Cinderella," *Peter Pan,* and *Abe Lincoln Grows Up,* though originating in different times and places and dissimilar in many ways, have one thing in common:

68

they all have archetypal characteristics. The archetypes embodied in such films as *The Wizard of Oz* and *Star Wars* may help to account for their continuing popularity. Similarly, the archetypal characteristics perceived in a person's life story may be what make that life a suitable subject for biography.

A knowledge of certain basic archetypes of character and plot may be useful for the study of biography, since they illustrate the characteristics of heroes, their relationships with others, and the underlying structure of their lives. The examples that follow are drawn from various mythological, literary, and historical sources, both to show the universality of archetypes and to demonstrate an archetypal approach to biography, specifically the life of Lincoln.

Character Archetypes

The Hero and the Villain are character archetypes that appear in all kinds of stories—from children's fairy tales to Western movies. The Hero often wears a white hat (or rides a white horse) and the Villain a black one. The colors, like the characters, are archetypal symbols for good and evil. In *Star Wars,* Luke Skywalker, whose name recalls the frequent association of mythological heroes with the sky, appears as the Hero dressed in white, with Darth Vader, his opponent, in black.

The Great Mother—or Earth Mother—is associated, like Ceres, with fertility. She is kind, good, and nurturing, in contrast to the Terrible Mother, who is cruel, tempting, and faithless. In *The Wizard of Oz,* Aunt Em, a Great Mother figure, loves and cares for Dorothy; as a Kansas farmer she is directly associated with the earth's fertility. Miss Gulch, a Terrible Mother figure, who steals Dorothy's dog Toto, appears later in the film version as the Wicked Witch of the West.

A third set of character archetypes illustrates complementary male-female relationships. A male character may represent the masculine part of a female personality, and vice versa. Jungian psychology gives the names *animus* and *anima* to these figures. In stories like "Cinderella" and "Sleeping Beauty," the animus is the prince or dream husband, the knight on a white charger who rescues the princess from the clutches of a villain or a witch. Or the relationship can be brotherly: in *The Wizard of Oz,* Dorothy is accompanied by three animus figures, the Scarecrow, the Tin Woodsman, and the Lion. The feminine counterpart of the animus, the anima, often appears in fairy tales as the princess whom the hero marries. In other stories she may be his ideal female, his soulmate, like Wendy in *Peter Pan.* Hansel and Gretel are a perfectly balanced pair, functioning as animus and anima for each other.

These literary examples have a certain simplicity of outline that historical personages lack; nevertheless, many real persons important to the subjects of biographies may have archetypal characteristics which are emphasized by the biographers or which emerge from a careful reading. For example, Sarah Bush Lincoln, Abe's stepmother, is a Great Mother figure, who cares for Abe and his brother and sisters. Maya Angelou's grandmother, Momma Henderson, is another Earth Mother figure, one who is a mother surrogate not only for Maya and Bailey but also for the entire black population of Stamps, Arkansas. Maya's brother Bailey is her animus; his personality complements hers, and he understands her as no one else does.

Plot Archetypes

Particularly applicable to the study of biography is the narrative archetype known as the Quest of the Hero. Sometimes known as the *monomyth,* it is central in the mythology and literature of widely differing cultures around the world. Its prevalence exemplifies the human need to believe in greatness and to have heroes—whether real or created. In the case of historical figures, the greatness of someone whose accomplishments exceed those of ordinary people seems to demand explanation, and so that person's story is told—for others to admire, to identify with, and to emulate. The subject of a biography must always be, in some sense, a hero to the biographer and the writing of a biography thus an act of hero-worship. Biographers tend to emphasize, consciously or unconsciously, the characteristics that emerge in the Quest of the Hero. This pattern undoubtedly runs deep in our collective unconscious.

Although the stages in the Quest of the Hero vary in number and in order of appearance, the basic outline of the story is the same, following the stages of a human life but emphasizing the exceptional qualities of the hero. The hero's life differs from an ordinary life primarily in the later stages, which deal with superhuman achievements and mythic significance. Of the six stages used here to demonstrate an archetypal approach to biography and to Lincoln's life, the first three emphasize physical and intellectual achievements; the last three emphasize—often in a symbolic way—spiritual triumphs and societal significance.

Miraculous Birth

The first stage of the pattern is a miraculous birth of some kind. Because it may seem impossible to believe that heroes can be born of ordinary people in the ordinary way, mythology and legend often attribute to them

royal or divine parentage: Theseus is a king's son; Achilles' mother is the
nymph Thetis; Helen of Troy is the daughter of Zeus. The circumstances
of heroes' conception or birth may also be unusual: Zeus comes to Helen's
mother Leda as a swan; the Buddha is conceived when a white elephant
circles his mother's couch; Athena is born by springing fully-armed from
her father's forehead. Some recent heroes are "born," like Superman and
E.T., by coming to Earth from remote planets, or are created, like the
Hulk, by an error in a scientific experiment.

Lincoln's birth is miraculous perhaps only because he survives it, given
the primitive conditions under which it takes place. His rustic upbringing,
however, recalls literary heroes like Oedipus and Perdita, royal children
adopted by poor shepherds and brought up in humble surroundings.
Heroes, whatever their genealogy, must have links with the common
people. Being born in a log cabin, like Lincoln, and growing up outside
the mainstream of civilization have almost become archetypes for the
American hero, expressing the significance of the frontier experience in
our national consciousness.

Sandburg emphasizes Lincoln's qualities as a folk hero in the details of
his early environment, devoting a whole chapter to the folk beliefs and
customs that surround young Abe. He enlarges the context by also relating the stories of Johnny Appleseed, another folk hero associated with
the earth, and of Henry Clay and Andrew Jackson, political heroes of the
"plain people."

Early Signs of Greatness

Mythological heroes demonstrate early the powers that are to make them
great. The baby Hercules strangles a snake in each hand. Atalanta,
brought up by a bear, shows early prowess at running and hunting. King
Arthur pulls the sword Excalibur from a stone when no one else can.
Siegfried kills a dragon and bathes in its blood. In biographies, where the
supernatural element is absent, this stage may be represented by the
biographer as the signs of talent a subject shows for a particular activity
or the emergence of the intellectual or artistic gifts that point toward
future success.

Sandburg demonstrates Abe Lincoln's early heroic potential through
anecdotes. Abe can fell trees like three men; he is a champion "rassler";
he throws out of the ring a bully who is beating up his stepbrother. In
one incident, he moves a whole corn-crib on his back while four men
with poles stand by useless. Abe also demonstrates high moral principles.
He pulls fodder for two days to pay for a borrowed book ruined by
rain. He rescues a drunk everyone else would have abandoned. He argues
against cruelty to animals. Abe's intellectual powers are also great, devel-

oped by conscientious self-education, since his formal schooling amounts to only about four months out of his life. He reads at the plough or at lunch. He listens avidly and absorbs stories from all kinds of people. When alone, he puzzles over words, over proverbs, over difficult questions. Lincoln's greatness, Sandburg implies, is the result of his possessing many fine physical, moral, and intellectual qualities, developed to an exceptional degree.

Period of Preparation

An important part of the Quest of the Hero is the period of preparation, characterized by experience, by withdrawal, or by education. King Arthur, as a child, becomes a bird and a fish with the help of Merlin the magician. Mohammed meditates in the cave of Hira. The Buddha receives supreme enlightenment sitting under the Bo tree. In Shakespeare's *Henry IV,* Prince Hal, with the help of Sir John Falstaff, undergoes many experiences that put him in touch with the lives of his future subjects. Unlike Prince Hal, Lincoln does not know in his youth exactly what he is preparing for. Nor do most historical figures. But most biographies include such a period of preparation or education, even though it may be unrecognized as such until later. Malcolm X spends several years "living by his wits" before discovering his vocation as a minister for the Nation of Islam. Marie Curie focuses steadily on her scientific education, preparing for her eventual discovery of radium. A biographer, looking at the subject's life in retrospect, typically details those experiences that obviously have led to the subject's later known achievements.

In *Abe Lincoln Grows Up,* Sandburg emphasizes particularly Abe's zest for "eddication," which is so strong that he counts as his best friend "the man who'll git me a book I ain't read." Among the books Abe reads in his youth are Aesop's Fables, the Bible, *Pilgrim's Progress,* and Weems's *Life of Washington.* By citing these particular books, Sandburg foreshadows Lincoln's later use of stories and fables in his speeches, his passion for justice and right action, and his stature as a hero ranking with Washington in national esteem. Sandburg also shows how Abe develops his rhetorical skills by offering his services as an amanuensis to illiterate neighbors, paying special attention to purpose, audience, and style as he helps them write their letters. The skills thus developed serve Lincoln well in his later legal experience, which may also be considered part of his period of preparation.

The Quest

Toward the end of *Abe Lincoln Grows Up,* Abe takes a trip down the Mississippi River to New Orleans. Journeys in mythology commonly signify passing from one stage of life to another; so it is with Lincoln. The journey marks three important transitions in his life: it symbolizes his passage from childhood to adulthood; it takes him from the context of his family and small rural community into the larger context of American urban life; and, by introducing him to the horrors of seeing slaves sold at auction, it foreshadows his long battle against the inhumane practice of slavery, a point deliberately made by Sandburg.

While mythological journeys usually have a specific purpose, such as founding a new Troy or discovering the Holy Grail, historical heroes rarely have such specific quests. They do achieve greatness, but only in retrospect are they invested with the fulfillment of a mission. Lincoln no doubt did not prepare himself specifically to become president, or to free the slaves, or to hold the union together—nor was he solely responsible for these achievements—but popular imagination has given him credit for them.

If *Abe Lincoln Grows Up* is read as a self-contained work, Abe's journey down the Mississippi may be considered his quest, his voyage of discovery. But if the events of the work are considered as only part of the larger whole of his life, then this journey is part of his period of preparation, and the achievements that culminate in the term of his presidency comprise his quest.

Death and Descent to the Underworld

Just as heroes' births are unusual, setting them apart from others, so their deaths are also unusual. They may lack burial, like King Arthur, whose body is floated down the river on a raft; or their graves may be unknown, like those of Moses and Cochise. Accompanying, or sometimes preceding, the hero's death may be a descent into the underworld, common to many heroes: Odysseus, Aeneas, Orpheus, and Proserpine from classical mythology, and also Moses, according to Jewish legend, and many Oriental, Polynesian, and American Indian figures. Heroes, however, return from the underworld, as ordinary mortals do not. These myths and legends symbolize the universal desire to triumph over death and the need to believe that heroes have actually done so.[1]

Heroes' triumphs are often achieved at great cost. They may become scapegoats, suffering and dying for their people. Oedipus is blinded—a symbolic death—but Thebes is purged. Proserpine must be dead to her mother for half the year in order to restore fertility to Earth. Prometheus is tortured, but the fire he has stolen benefits mankind.

Such motifs are heavily mythical and thus not found literally in biographies. They do, however, often appear symbolically, emphasizing the subjects' spiritual triumphs. Symbolic death occurs when heroes lose some of the powers that have made them great. A Glenn Cunningham who cannot run is still Glenn Cunningham, but Glenn Cunningham the runner is dead. So it is with others: Beethoven becomes deaf; Curie's eyesight fails; Jill Kinmont is paralyzed. Some historical heroes also take on a scapegoat function. Luther, excommunicated, is dead in the eyes of the church; Galileo is forced to recant his theories; but the causes for which these heroes suffer are not lost.

During such times of crisis, subjects may be plunged into depths of despair, a symbolic descent to the underworld. They may be tortured by their impotence: Curie struggles to read her notes, using thick, powerful lenses; Beethoven writes music he will never hear performed; Luthei languishes in prison. Heroes know many dark nights of the soul.

In Lincoln's death we can see a powerful combination of these motifs. He may be considered a scapegoat for the American people, the sacrificial hero cut down in his prime to expiate the sin of slavery. The hours after his shooting by Booth are a symbolic descent into hell, an agony for him and for the country. He also lacks burial, at least during the time his body is taken on a tour for the country to mourn. This ceremonial journey, hardly a common funeral practice, underlines his heroic stature.

Resurrection, Atonement, Apotheosis

The final stages of the quest archetype emphasize heroes victory over death and their immortality. Mythological heroes are resurrected, like Osiris, or return from the underworld periodically, like Proserpine, or become part of nature—Adonis as a tree, Hercules as a constellation. In biographies, just as symbolic death takes many forms, so does symbolic resurrection. Jill Kinmont finds another vocation, teaching; Glenn Cunningham learns to run again; Luther founds a new church. More important perhaps, heroic individuals learn to accept what they cannot change, thus achieving atonement with power greater than their own. Apotheosis may come when heroes are literally canonized, like Joan of Arc, or idealized, like Gandhi, John F. Kennedy, and Martin Luther King, Jr. More often it comes when their ideas are accepted, as with Galileo, or when their works are recognized, as with Dickinson. Many artists and scientists, too original to be part of the mainstream in their own lifetimes, are canonized years, perhaps even centuries, later. This represents a symbolic atonement with society and with tradition.

Although not literally resurrected, Lincoln is still very much alive. In the more than a century since his death, he has become permanently accepted as one of our greatest presidents. The political opposition he knew in his own day, exemplified by Booth, has long since faded away; he is at one with the tradition of American history. We Americans continue to admire his virtues and revere his accomplishments. Lincoln has come as close to being deified as any American hero.

All societies have created heroes, admired their accomplishments, and told their stories. Although greatness has been explained in many ways, ranging from the supernatural events of mythological explanations to the genetic programming of modern scientific ones, the desire for explanation has not changed. Biographers, when writing about a subject, consciously or unconsciously emphasize traits to meet certain basic expectations—theirs and their audience's. If they exaggerate some traits and overlook or downplay others, it is no doubt because of the need, buried deep in our collective unconscious, to find—or to create—heroic models.

Note

1. We have not used the story of Jesus in any of our examples, although it corresponds at every point with the archetype of the Quest of the Hero. In a multicultural public school classroom, it would probably be equally unproductive to treat the story either as just a myth like any other myth or as *the* literal and absolute truth. Although "myth" has a precise scholarly meaning, in popular usage it is often equated with falsehood. Students who are troubled by the use of this word in connection with their most deeply held religious beliefs may be helped by having it pointed out to them, as a teacher of one of the authors once did to her, that there can be "truth of idea" as well as "truth of fact." Truth of idea can be expressed in myth, metaphor, and other non-literal ways, but it is no less valid and valuable than truth of fact. The story of Jesus, embodying both kinds of truth, makes Jesus a very great hero indeed.

Guidelines for Using the Archetypal Approach

1. Place events of the subject's life on a line from birth to death. Can you find events or periods that correspond with stages in the hero myth? What is the "hero's quest" in this work? What is the hero's symbolic experience of death and descent into the underworld? Are these experiences emphasized by archetypal symbols, colors, or motifs?

2. On the line of events constructed above, divide the subject's life into stages in a day, into seasons of the year. Do these stages correspond with each other? With the hero myth?

3. Considering the subject as hero, are there other persons or forces that can be identified as villain, anima, animus, Great Mother, Terrible Mother? What characteristics do they possess that suggest their association with these archetypes?

4. Find a scene in the work that is significant as a turning point in the life of the subject. Is there any symbolism of setting (such as forest or desert) or any reference to seasons or times of day (such as a sunset foreshadowing death) that might enhance the archetypal significance of the event? Are there colors, such as black or red, that may symbolize evil or passion? (Not every significant scene will be archetypal, of course, but looking for such clues can often be rewarding.)

Classroom Applications of "The Power of Myth: An Archetypal Approach"

1. Make a lifeline for a typical person, based on the analogy of a day, putting in the ages at which a person reaches each stage. Compare the teacher's example with those of several students, e.g.:

	Morning	Noon	Afternoon	Evening	Night
Teacher	Birth	Age 40	Age 65	Age 80	Death
Student A	Birth	Age 21	Age 35	Age 45	Death
Student B	Age 2	Age 30	Age 50	Age 70	Death

   Fill in spaces on the line with significant events in the person's life. Create a line for Lincoln's life. How does it compare with the teacher's? the students'? At what point on the line does *Abe Lincoln Grows Up* end?

2. Do the same thing, using the analogy of seasons of the year. What differences are evident?

3. Many common figures of speech exemplify archetypes of the day or of the season: "the prime of life," "put to sleep," "the springtime of youth." Can you find examples of such figures in *Abe Lincoln Grows Up*?

4. Do important events in *Abe Lincoln Grows Up* happen at times of day or seasons of the year that may have archetypal significance? If so, have these times or seasons been emphasized by Sandburg?

5. Does Sandburg use colors in a way that may have archetypal significance? Find examples and comment on them.

6. Does Sandburg emphasize archetypal settings, such as wilderness, river, city? If so, what is their significance?

7. Make two lists, one of famous heroes, including Lincoln, and one of famous villains. What characteristics do the heroes share? the villains? Can you identify a villain or villains in *Abe Lincoln Grows Up*? In Lincoln's later life?

8. Choose a famous person whom you admire. Compare the events in that person's life with the stages of the Quest of the Hero. How does the life resemble Lincoln's? How does it differ?

9. Write about a symbolic death, descent to the underworld, and resurrection experienced by you or someone you know.

10. Write the life story of a fictitious person, using the stages of the hero myth. This can also be done in groups, with one person or group responsible for each stage, passing it on to the next when completed.

Persona and Persuasion:
A Rhetorical Approach

Sandra Johnson Treharne

"What do you want to say in the letter? How do you want to say it? Are you sure that's the best way to say it? Or do you think we can fix up a better way to say it?"

—Abe Lincoln Grows Up

Rhetoric aims to manipulate an audience through language. Orators manipulate listeners with verbal persuasiveness; writers control readers with literary devices. From the first phase of any literary work, fiction or nonfiction, the reader explores a world of language with the narrator as guide. The narrator assumes a certain posture or personality called a *persona*. This persona speaks to the reader from a certain perspective or point of view; its voice conveys a tone toward the reader and attitude toward the subject matter. The words the narrator chooses, the way those words are arranged in sentences, and the way those sentences are arranged in the work have a cumulative effect in forming a fictional world. How believable that world is depends entirely upon the writer's rhetorical skills.

In all literature, rhetorical skill involves a writer's ability to interweave the classical elements of narration, incident, character, and setting into a textual unity. But to achieve such unity is more than just imaginative prose; rather, it is the "achieved effect," the controlled arrangement of language. A rhetorical evaluation considers both the intent and effectiveness of such devices in a literary text; it seeks to discover how a piece of writing works, and why it works that way.

In biography and autobiography, narration operates much the way it does in fiction: there is a story to be told and the events of that story occur in some kind of time frame. In both genres, narration inherently involves a "double life." Events "happened" once and they are being "retold" by the narrator. This perspective is especially relevant in autobiography because events happened in a historic time frame and now "happen" in a rhetorical time frame. Another point to consider with biography and autobiography is the principle of selective recall. A writer of autobiography like Maya Angelou makes conscious selections of what to tell readers about the past. She cannot, obviously, narrate all the events of her life. Therefore, she picks and chooses incidents to serve her narrational needs. The ability to relate events and emotions selectively to achieve an ultimate effect is a fundamental principle of rhetorical skill. It is the reason behind the rhetoric. If a piece of writing "works," successfully persuading readers to see, feel, and experience as the author intended, then the components of rhetorical art have achieved textual unity.

Perspective and Persona in *I Know Why the Caged Bird Sings*

Maya Angelou's *I Know Why the Caged Bird Sings* is an effective piece of writing because it achieves such unity. By the end of the text, readers believe Angelou to be the woman she believes herself to be, a formidable black American who has survived the "tripartite crossfire of masculine prejudice, white illogical hate and Black lack of power." Somehow, Angelou has persuaded the reader to a position of empathy. How she achieves this success is a question rhetorical analysis tries to answer.

If empathy is the rhetorical intent of *I Know Why the Caged Bird Sings,* the effectiveness of the text seems to rest upon two principles of narrational control. The first is Angelou's ability to recall and relate incidents from her past that move readers to an understanding of her life, as she chooses to have them know it. Readers, of course, have no way of knowing the veracity of these recollections; indeed, whether they are actually "true" or not has little relevance to the text. What is relevant is her ability to convey the impression of the "real thing," to give the reader patterns from which to guess the whole of experience. For example, in the few paragraphs of the book's introduction, Angelou conveys the sense of a child who feels somehow deprived, a child who has known rejection, punishment, repression, and release. Such selection of incident serves to illustrate the whole of her experience.

Just as important is Angelou's selection of persona. Autobiography can be seen as having the double life mentioned before, but from a single person's perspective; Angelou's perspective is one of recollection. Certain things happened to her once and she relates them to the reader in retrospect. This is her starting point. Since she is now a grown woman, the perspective on the past of Maya the adult is colored by years of growth and experience. The persona that emerges from this point of view assumes a stance or attitude of judgmental detachment:

> To be left alone on the tightrope of youthful unknowing is to experience the excruciating beauty of full freedom and the threat of eternal indecision. Few, if any, survive their teens. Most surrender

> to the vague but murderous pressure of adult conformity. It becomes
> easier to die and avoid conflicts than to maintain a constant battle
> with the superior forces of maturity. (231)

It is a polished voice that makes generalizations and sums up entire eras:

> . . . each generation found it more expedient to plead guilty to the
> charge of being young and ignorant, easier to take the punishment
> meted out by the older generation. . . . The command to grow up at
> once was more bearable than the faceless horror of wavering pur-
> pose, which was youth. (231)

This persona sees itself as a spokesperson for a generation, capable of
objective criticism; it is caustically and carefully persuasive. It makes
readers believe its rhetoric through its very self-control and alleged objectivity. As the narrative unfolds, however, the reader will recognize a
voice that does not sound like this eloquent grown woman. Indeed, it
becomes evident from the very first page that there is another very strong
voice at work, the voice of a bewildered child. This persona sees adults as
the enemy; it lacks confidence, begs for assurance:

> Could I tell her now? The terrible pain assured me that I couldn't.
> What he did to me, and what I allowed must have been very bad if
> already God let me hurt so much. If Mr. Freeman was gone, did
> that mean Bailey was out of danger? And if so, if I told him, would
> he still love me? (68)

This is clearly another voice, and it is that of Ritie the child. Often, in the
power of a scene, the two voices merge in a single paragraph: "I sat with
my family (Bailey couldn't come) and they rested still on the seats like
solid, cold gray tombstones. Thick and forevermore unmoving" (70).
More frequently, the two voices work in juxtaposition to heighten effect.
To Ritie the child, events seem to be "occurring," whereas for Maya the
adult the events have already "occurred." Readers are, in effect, allowed
the subjectivity and the immediacy of an event, as well as given the benefit
of Maya's more objective adult perspective of memory and summation.
The switch from adult to child seems to serve one particular end: it forces
the reader to feel acutely how Ritie felt when the incident happened. Only
the child could so poignantly say, "From the way he was holding me I
knew he'd never let me go or let anything bad ever happen to me. This
was probably my real father and we had found each other at last" (61).
This plaintive voice is the same one that can take the reader back to the
feeling of wetting one's pants, the immediacy of the moment when

> a green persimmon, or it could have been a lemon, caught me
> between the legs and squeezed. I tasted the sour on my tongue and
> felt it in the back of my mouth. Then before I reached the door, the
> sting was burning down my legs and into my Sunday socks. (3)

No refined adult persona could convey the immediacy of such a moment. The reader is indebted to Ritie the child for the deepest insights into the experiences of childhood. If the persona had spoken only from the adult perspective, the effect would have been lost. This is what is meant by an achieved effect, or artful combination of image, technique, and arrangement by the writer to manipulate reader response.

Persona and Reader

The relationship between persona and reader differs with each shift in persona. Ritie shares intimacies with the reader as close friends do. Yet she does not hesitate to assault the reader with truth. If things hurt, she makes the reader feel the hurt:

> Later Mother made a broth and sat on the edge of the bed to feed me. The liquid went down my throat like bones. My belly and behind were as heavy as cold iron, but it seemed my head had gone away and pure air had replaced it. (67)

Ritie's language explodes with metaphors and similes as if she is desperately trying to convey the "is" of the "was." She picks her words with care and fashions them into delicate phrases: "the dress I wore was lavender taffeta and each time I breathed, it rustled"; colorfully clever phrases: "old-lady-long," and "her long yellow face was full of sorry"; and poignant phrases: "I pictured his mouth pulling down on the right side and his saliva flowing into the eyes of new potatoes." She reveals character in a few well-chosen sentences. In a terse paragraph, the reader meets—and knows—Mrs. Flowers:

> Her skin was a rich black that would have peeled like a plum if snagged, but then no one would have thought of getting close enough to Mrs. Flowers to ruffle her dress, let alone snag her skin. She didn't encourage familiarity. She wore gloves, too. (78)

Uncle Tommy "was never cruel. He was mean." And Sister Monroe "stood in front of the altar, shaking like a freshly caught trout." The persona that shares these images makes the reader see and feel as she herself sees and feels. Ritie is the imaginative writer, who, like the Reverend Thomas, "[throws] out phrases like home-run balls." Hers is a passionate, poetic voice that weeps and laughs and, most significantly, portrays the past as no other voice could.

The adult persona persuades on another level. In contrast to Ritie, Maya the adult speaks with reserve; she editorializes; she rejects familiarity with the reader. Hers is the controlled voice of an adult which, though full of conviction, insists on a professional distance from her readers. If

Ritie moves readers more through immediacy and emotion, Maya moves her readers primarily through intellect. Yet, even this adult voice can persuade through the emotions. In sophisticated rhetoric, she speaks not only for herself as a black woman but for a generation of black people who struggled, and suffered, and survived:

> Oh, Black known and unknown poets, how often have your auctioned pains sustained us? Who will compute the lonely nights made less lonely by your songs, or the empty pots made less tragic by your tales?
>
> If we were a people much given to revealing secrets, we might raise monuments and sacrifice to the memories of our poets, but slavery cured us of that weakness. (156)

Her rhetoric is both persuasive and poetic; it is also tough, streetwise, and polished to an icy brilliance. This is the persona that has survived Ritie's past, and endures: "I had outdistanced unpleasant sensations by miles. I was headed for the freedom of open fields" (145). Functioning as editor, this resolute persona pulls the narrative together, organizes it, then pushes it along. This voice opens and closes chapters and tells the reader facts. It is the cohesive force throughout the text, summing up Ritie's emotional responses, categorizing and evaluating life.

The juxtaposition of voices works to make the text believable. For example, in the progression of events in the molestation scene and after a general introduction concerning life with Mother and Mr. Freeman in St. Louis, the adult persona rationalizes Ritie's habit of sleeping in her mother's bed, saying, "Because of a need for stability, children easily become creatures of habit" (60). Immediately following this "conclusion," Ritie the child tells of the first sexual overture by Mr. Freeman:

> It was too soft to be a hand, and it wasn't the touch of clothes. . . .
> It didn't move, and I was too startled to. . . . I knew, as if I had always known, it was his "thing" on my leg. (60)

This passage alternates between the expressive emotionalism of Ritie's voice and the controlled commentary of Maya the adult. Ritie's voice is unsure; it questions the reality of the situation. Maya the adult, however, returns to rescue the reader from any ambiguity. She confirms the child's experience with mature rhetoric. The little girl shows; the adult tells.

Synthesis and Resolution

As the text moves from the childhood to the adulthood of Maya Angelou, the voices of Ritie the child and Maya the adult begin to merge into a kind of synthesis of youth and age, childishness and wisdom. Rather than the deftly delineated paragraphs of the first half of the book, the two personas seem to grow together to form a new voice. The most natural of the three voices of *I Know Why the Caged Bird Sings,* it can unabashedly exclaim, in a vernacular phrase that Maya the adult would never have permitted: "It be's like that sometimes" (191). In fact, this voice emerges only after the terrible events of Angelou's childhood have been divulged by Ritie and then editorialized and assimilated by Maya. This emergent persona—synthesis of pain and promise, poignancy and polish—greets the reader with a dose of reality, and, what's more, with the wisdom of a newfound sense of humor.

The transition occurs almost simultaneously with Ritie's graduation from grammar school (chapter 23). Having achieved the status of "person of the moment," and one of the top students in the graduating class, Ritie seems to emerge from a cocoon of bitterness—if not as a butterfly, at least as a moth who "was going to be lovely." Suddenly, the persona achieves a sense of worth, as if it had been gained as a result of having revealed the incidents of an agonizing childhood:

> Youth and social approval allied themselves with me and we trammeled memories of slights and insults. The wind of our swift passage remodeled my features. Lost tears were pounded to mud and then to dust. Years of withdrawal were brushed aside and left behind. (145)

Her hair pleases her, her dress pleases her; indeed, she graduates into an entirely new era, as well as into a new life in San Francisco (chapter 26). Her voice, emerging from the agony of years of withdrawal, guilt, and pain, has an integrity all its own. It somehow reconciles the past with the present; it is the self which, growing as a person, discovers humor and finds life acceptable. At their late-night party in San Francisco, she realizes that

> there was nothing for it but to laugh at our beautiful and wild mother. . . .
> We were served formally, and she apologized for having no orchestra to play for us but said she'd sing as a substitute. She sang and did the Time Step and the Snake Hips and the Suzy Q. What child can resist a mother who laughs freely and often, especially if the child's wit is mature enough to catch the sense of the joke? (174)

Angelou continues to move forward with assurance, dignity, and her child's maturing wit. And, although there are more "terrible things" to relate from author to reader, the "sour" is gone. Ritie the child has reached reconciliation with Maya the adult; the result is a whole person.

Guidelines for Using the Rhetorical Approach

Every piece of discourse has a speaker (or a persona), an audience, and a subject. While it is usually easy to identify the subject—at least on a superficial level—the characteristics of the speaker and the audience must often be inferred from clues in the text.

The character of the speaker in a work of fiction may be relatively easy to identify; for instance, in *Huckleberry Finn* it is the twelve-year-old Huck whose voice we "hear," not that of the author. Although in other works author and speaker may be less easy to separate, the speaker's voice should not be automatically identified with the author's. Even in an autobiography, where the author and the speaker are the same person, there may be two or more different voices—that of the child or younger person who underwent the experiences recounted and the adult voice commenting upon them in retrospect.

The characteristics of the audience to which the writer is appealing may be even more difficult to pin down, but critical examination of the text will usually furnish abundant evidence from which to draw inferences.

1. Look at the first page of the work. Is the story told in first person or in third? If it is third person, what relationship does the speaker have with the subject of the biography? Is the subject someone the biographer has known personally or someone about whom evidence has been collected? Does the biographer's own experience form part of the narrative? When recounting events, does the speaker seem to know what the subject is thinking or to rely more on objective evidence? What is the attitude toward the subject, as shown, for instance, by the use of evaluative adjectives? (See "From the Inside Out: A Linguistic Approach.") In an autobiography, does the narrative begin with the child's voice recounting an experience or the adult voice supplying facts and comments? Is there a shift between two voices? Where can that shift be detected?

2. What audience does the work appear to be written for? Some clues that might determine the age and reading ability of an audience are sentence length, difficulty of vocabulary, or complexity of sentence structure (see "From the Inside Out"). Are there incidents or statements that would not be accepted by certain audiences—for example, racist, sexist, or anti-youth remarks? Works are often classified as "women's books," or as "young adult." What are the assumptions about those audiences that lead to classifications like these? Does the speaker expect the audience to agree with certain assumptions—for instance, that the normal family is WASP and

consists of father, mother, and two children, or that the expected behavior for a young woman is to follow the traditional pattern of centering her life on and deferring to the opinions and lead of a man?

3. On the surface, the subject of a biography or autobiography is the life of a certain person. There may be, however, a more profound subject that can be identified by examining the work for "messages." For example, "If you work as hard as X, you can be successful." Try to isolate "load-bearing" passages in the work that sum up or reflect upon the subject's experience. What message does the work as a whole seem to have for readers?

4. The three major rhetorical appeals identified by Aristotle are the *rational,* the *emotional,* and the *ethical.*

   a. The *rational* appeal is to reason, to logic. Often it is possible to construct the syllogism implicit in a work:
      All persons are created equal.
      Blacks are persons.
      Therefore, blacks are equal to other persons.

   b. The *emotional* appeal is based on shared human values; for example, anger at mistreatment of a child, sorrow for an untimely death. What incidents in the work call forth strong emotions in the reader? What is the expected audience reaction? What values is it assumed the audience will share?

   c. The *ethical* appeal is the appeal of the persona as a person, someone the audience can like or trust or admire. An audience that reacts favorably to a speaker will more readily accept that speaker's message. Is the speaker in this work likable, admirable, trustworthy? Try to identify places in the work where the speaker or another character uses an ethical appeal. Does the speaker as presented throughout the work come across as the kind of person whose message is believable? Has the speaker persuaded you to change your mind about any beliefs you may have had previously?

Classroom Applications of "Persona and Persuasion: A Rhetorical Approach"

1. Find passages from the text in which Maya the adult sums up and categorizes an experience she described as Ritie the child. For example, "High spots in Stamps were usually negative: droughts, floods, lynchings and deaths" (76). Discuss whether the incident

described sufficiently illustrates the "summing-up" sentence. Find other passages in the persona of Maya that serve as topic sentences, supported by Ritie's experience.

2. Read the last paragraphs of several chapters. Is the persona that of Maya or of Ritie? How can you tell?

3. Find an example of a passage in which Ritie persuades the reader through emotional appeal. Then find a passage in which Maya persuades through reason, or an appeal to the intellect. What is each persona trying to persuade the reader of? Which persona is more effective? Why?

4. What does the book as a whole seem to be trying to persuade the reader of? In what ways is this autobiography effective as a persuasive text? In what ways does it fail to persuade? Is there a "hidden meaning" in the work, a deeper message than just the telling of Angelou's life story?

5. Is there a different message in this book for whites and for blacks? What audience is Angelou primarily writing for? What age level? Which sex?

6. What kind of person is Angelou? How does she establish herself as a believable narrator and a worthy person by means of ethical appeal?

7. Choose a passage from the work describing an incident in Angelou's life. Rewrite the passage in the third person. What differences do you determine?

2 More Ideas for Using Biography and Autobiography

Judging a Book by Its Cover:
A Prereading Book Analysis

Jo McGinnis

One teacher I know regularly enlists the help of the school librarian to bring the library to the classroom. They select books to "sell" to students by means of book talks. She wheels in a cartload of volumes, both hard- and paperback, and passes them around the class at random, so that each person can hold one.

"Some of my students," she says, "never go to a library willingly, never have the sense of feeling the heft of books or opening them to smell the newness or mustiness. This approach seems to be a nonthreatening way to let them experience something that I find pleasurable."

She is also aware that her students are young consumers, subject to the marketing tricks of the advertising trade. As a result of these book talks, she is not only encouraging these young people to become familiar with books in general, but also to become knowledgeable about the selling tactics of the publishers who display their wares in the bookracks of drugstores and supermarkets. She is, in effect, showing them how to judge a book by its cover and its other "packaging" devices by means of a systematic, intentionally "superficial" analysis.

Some of her students are practiced artists at this kind of superficial book analysis, of course. They have been writing book reports for years based upon what they have read on the dustcovers of library books. The teacher who confronts this practice accomplishes two important objectives: first, the prereading analysis becomes valuable as an exercise in itself rather than as a means of "cheating" on a book report. Pages of writing can be generated from the questions a reader might ask about a book without reading more than a few lines of print. Second, the important difference is revealed between a book analysis based upon this prereading experience and a critical book review based upon what is inside the book's covers. The student knows that the teacher is aware of the difference and that there is a time for each kind of reporting, but that the two should not be confused. With these objectives in mind, then, the teacher may lead a class through the following suggested steps in deciding whether this is a book that sells its message effectively.

1. Describe the cover in terms of the elements used to attract attention and to establish a first impression. What colors are used to evoke what appeal? Does it use sex to attract attention? What audience does it hope to attract? Paperback romances, especially, use colors and illustrations in a stylized manner according to the intended audience. Stories for younger readers are packaged in white and pastel colors with "innocent" illustrations. The racier the romance, the stronger the color and images. Include at least one "bodice-buster" in red and black to illustrate the point, but warn students of the dangers of making generalizations too quickly, the dangers of judging a book by its cover.

2. Who is the author of the book? Is he, like Carl Sandburg, famous for other writing? Is she, like Maya Angelou, known for activities other than writing? Sometimes information about the author can be found inside the book's back cover. Somewhere around the title page, or on the book jacket, may be a list of other works by the author. Can the reader tell what experience or background qualifies the author to write about this particular subject?

3. If the hardcover edition has a jacket, compare it with the binding underneath. If hard- and softcover editions are available for the same book, compare the packaging of the two. Is there anything about the binding, the print, the white spaces, or the illustrations that adds to the aesthetic appeal of either edition?

4. As students open the book and leaf through the pages, they may describe their impressions. Is it a new book with pages as yet uncut? Or is it well used and "comfortable"? A little instruction on care and respect for books is appropriate at this point.

5. Who is the publisher of the book? Which publishers are most frequently named in the class? Point out that books are traditionally published first in hardback, but that hardbacks generally earn more prestige than money. If a book gets good reviews and sells well in hardback, it is then published in paperback. A real blockbuster may then sell to the movies. If the movie is popular, often a book will appear based upon the movie that was based upon the novel! All of this information may be found through close reading of the cover, the title page, and the copyright page. Most romances, westerns, and other "category" books are published in paperback only, however.

6. When was the book first published? Has it gone through several reprints? Is it in translation from another language? The copyright page offers a clue to "dated" material. Include, for example, a book on space written in the sixties; books focusing on areas of research and experimentation are quickly outdated. Point out, however, that good literature crosses time boundaries. In some works, an old copyright date indicates a continued popularity and wide appeal. Carl Sandburg's *Abe Lincoln Grows Up* is an example.

7. Look at the illustrations in the book. For economic reasons, paperbacks will have very few. Books for young readers, especially children's books, will have a much higher proportion of illustrations to print. Serious biographies may have photographs of the subject and may include maps, documents, and other representative material. Check the name of the illustrator. Is it a well-known one? Judgments about the scholarship involved in the work may be made from the evidence presented by the illustrations.

8. Look at the table of contents. If a work is a biography, how much of the subject's life does it cover? Are the chapter headings symbolic, or are they clear statements of what material is included?

9. How long is the work? Since many readers judge a book's readability from length alone, students will find this an important consideration.

10. Read the first paragraph. At what point in the subject's life does the biographer begin the story? If the work is fiction, does the first paragraph draw the reader immediately into the story? What is promised the reader in this first paragraph? If it doesn't promise quick action, skip to page 50 or 100 and sample another paragraph. Has the action picked up? Look for clues to the author's style and tone.

   Read the final paragraph. Some students may consider this cheating, but it is a valuable means of judging the scope of a book and determining the ideas of the author.

Based upon this decidedly superficial analysis, students will be able to make a more informed judgment about what the book promises. In the book talks that students will make to the class or in smaller groups, they may use this procedure to report their findings. The evidence gathered will give specific detail to support their personal evaluations. If a student feels no interest in reading the book, a guess may be made as to the intended audience. Is there someone else in the class who might like it?

Dealing with Sensitive Subjects

Randall Smith, Margaret Fleming, Jo McGinnis, and
Lindley Hunter Silverman

Of course, I knew that lots of people did "it" and that they used
their "things" to accomplish the deed. . . .

—*I Know Why the Caged Bird Sings*

At the age of eight, Maya Angelou was raped by her mother's boyfriend,
Mr. Freeman. She recounts this event in her autobiography, *I Know Why
the Caged Bird Sings*. She is neither dramatic nor euphemistic about it;
she merely tells us this fact of her life.

Maya describes Mr. Freeman's crime naturally and explicitly because
it is something that really happened. And Maya is just as forthright in
describing her reactions of guilt and shame and how she dealt with these
emotions.

It is unreasonable to believe that an adolescent reader could somehow
be harmed by reading Angelou's articulate story of her childhood, teenage
years, and growth into motherhood. The effect on the reader is more
likely to be shock, enlightenment, wonder, excitement, pleasure, empathy.

Young readers are willing to read, listen, and share feelings when they
have the opportunity to do so in a context where an open-minded teacher
shares their concerns. Such a teacher must also be knowledgeable about
the needs and characteristics of adolescents, understanding and tolerant
of their initial reactions to a sensitive subject like rape. The boys may
snicker and draw fantastic sexual organs inside textbook covers; the girls
may be mortally embarrassed. Then someone says, "Mr. Freeman de-
served to die," and the debate is on. Imagine. Young people seriously
arguing crime and punishment—and in the process learning from each
other.

The truth is that all human beings are sexual beings. Just because
students may be engrossed in reading about or discussing an episode such
as Maya's rape by her own mother's boyfriend does not mean that they
are unhappy with their own lives or eager to engage in illicit sexual or

92

violent activities. It is an indication, rather, of natural curiosity about events that are all around us in the everyday, real world.

Adolescents are typically curious, especially about anything related to sex. Surely it is better for them to learn about rape vicariously than the way Maya does. While all of us might prefer that children not know about rape at all, it is a fact of life in our society, at every level, and knowledge may be an effective preventive. If there should be students in the class who have suffered sexual violation—regrettably a real possibility—they may be helped to cope with their feelings by discovering that the same thing has happened to others.

Adolescents often feel alone. Reading provides a way for them to share in the common experiences of adolescence. In this case, the common experience is not the rape itself, but the reactions to it that Maya feels— guilt, humiliation, fear—reactions teenagers often have to any experience over which they have no control.

Adolescents often simply do not know enough. In a discussion of Maya's rape, for instance, the following misconceptions may surface: rape occurs only in certain segments of society; child abuse does not happen in educated families; rape is simply the result of sexual urges; rape is always invited by the victim. It is hard to imagine how an innocent eight-year-old could deliberately have provoked such an attack, yet in Maya's case, Mr. Freeman's attorney treats her as if she must somehow have been at fault. These and other myths about sexual experiences of all kinds can be dispelled by a knowledgeable teacher within the context of a discussion. It is important, however, always to keep such a discussion grounded in the text under consideration in order to provide the needed objectivity.

Teachers try to encourage their students to develop positive attitudes toward reading by recommending books that will help them cope with their moods, their emotions, and the problems of their own worlds. But as adolescents indulge in new interests and new reading experiences, parents may become frightened. "Rape," "pregnancy," "abortion," "drugs," glimpsed on book jackets, may trigger fears that send them rushing to schools and libraries to complain about what their children are being exposed to.

It is certainly understandable that parents want to protect their children from the feared effects of change—changes in environment and changes in the adolescents themselves. Teachers, however, have a responsibility to use that which literature offers them to protect students from the effects of their own ignorance. If a girl, for example, has been protected from the *knowledge* of seduction, how will she cope with the *act* of seduction?

There is no doubt that this question, like many others which deal frankly with sex, demands skillful handling by a sensitive teacher. But such questions need to be addressed when they arise from the context of literature. If skirted, they only provoke mistrust and promote ignorance on the part of our students. Think how differently most of us older teachers would feel about sexual topics in the classroom if, during our adolescence, some of the issues had been discussed in an open forum, with facts and literary examples to clarify this troublesome area.

One tough question still hangs in the air. How do teachers decide what to do with such books as Angelou's autobiography and the sexual frankness that is part of it? There are at least four choices:

1. Don't let students read the book. See that it is kept out of the classroom and the library. Better keep it out of the bookstore too.

2. Tell students they shouldn't read the book. They are not old enough. Their parents would object. (At least this way the book gets read.)

3. Recommend the book for outside reading for those students who appear to be mature enough to handle it, offering to discuss it with any students who have questions or ideas to bring up.

4. Read and discuss the book in class.

The first three alternatives are safe. The last is risky. Risks, however, can be overcome, and the rewards are worth it. Confront the outbursts and struggle with the ugly subjects raised. Patiently withstand the awkward silences. Remember that the text is always a refuge. Not every question will be asked, or need be answered. This can be an exciting learning experience and an opportunity to treat adolescents with respect, an opportunity that should not be avoided.

Writing Assignments Focusing on Autobiographical and Biographical Topics

Margaret Fleming

"When I Was Born"

Go to the library and find a copy of a newspaper published the day you were born. What was the headline? What were the big stories nationally? internationally? What was happening in politics? in athletics? in entertainment? What can you tell from the ads about jobs, wages, and prices?

In your home town, what was the important front-page news? If you can't find a local newspaper, interviewing parents or older adults may be helpful in getting this information. Find out from parents what was happening in your own family.

Select items of interest from the information you have collected, arrange them in a way to catch a reader's interest, and write a brief piece that will give a sense of what things were like when you were born.

Variation: Do this for another person's birthday—a parent, a brother or sister, a grandparent. It would make an original birthday gift for anyone

Letter to a Newborn Baby

Pretend you are your mother or your father at the time of your birth, and write a letter to the newborn baby (you), introducing the family and telling the newcomer what's going on in the world and what to expect in the weeks and months ahead.

A Sensory Experience

Think of an experience from your early life in which one or more of your senses were intensely involved. Make lists under the headings SIGHT, SOUND, TASTE, SMELL, TOUCH. Which sense impressions are most vivid, as you recall them? Write a description of the experience or of the place where it happened, trying to recreate for your reader these vivid sensory impressions.

"My Life Box"

Choose three objects that you would put into a box to symbolize what is important in your life. Describe each object briefly and tell what it means to you. You may want to describe the box also.

A Memorable Object

Choose an object that is important to you because it reminds you of a certain person or a certain experience. Describe the object physically and then recall the characteristics of the person or the experience it reminds you of.

An Influential Person

Think of a person who had an important influence on your life. How did you first meet this person? What do you remember of your first impressions? What experiences did you share with this person? How was this person's influence felt? Does it continue to be felt? What do you remember best about this person?

A Fictionalized Biographical Incident

Tell a story about something that happened to someone you know. If you don't know all the details, you may have to invent such things as conversation and thoughts that fit the person's character, even though you have no way of knowing what actually was said or thought.

Begin with the opening situation. Tell what happened to start a conflict or create a problem. What did the person do? How was the conflict resolved or the problem solved? What, if anything, happened after that?

Variation: Write a story about one of your parents, as if you were telling it to a young child of your own. Be sure to use words that a child could understand.

A Dramatized Biographical Incident

Write a short play about an incident in the life of someone in your family. If you have heard the story from others, you may have to invent specific conversations and other details that weren't mentioned.

Start by describing where the action takes place—date, time, place, whether inside or outside, etc. Then have your main character (parent, grandparent, cousin) interact with one or more other persons. Try to include in the dialogue as many facts as necessary for understanding the story (e.g., "Don't point your finger at me"; "Those clouds look like rain"). You may also use stage directions to indicate movement and facial gestures.

As in the fictionalized incident, include an opening situation (necessarily brief), the introduction of a problem or conflict, and a resolution.

Note: This assignment would be appropriate after a class had studied drama and learned some of its techniques and terminology.

The Biography Kit

Lindley Hunter Silverman

Every time I finish reading a biography I say, "I want to write one!"
Immediately I begin to contemplate the demands of such a project. First I
think about the herculean requirements of a good biographer: the dedica-
tion of a generalist, the expertise of a specialist, the enthusiasm of an
adventurer, and the curiosity of a detective. Then I envision the thousands
of pieces of information that must be found and fitted together to "represent" that remarkable work of art: a life lived. Then I ponder the time
and effort required to complete such an undertaking.

The last time I rehearsed this sequence of thoughts, I was just
approaching the point of being completely overwhelmed by the immensity
of the task when I realized I had been overlooking the fact that in my
English classroom I had at least thirty research assistants for a biography
project. Using our combined abilities as generalists, specialists, adven-
turers, and detectives, we could collectively "research" and write the
biography of a person of our own creation. This idea was the genesis of
the Biography Kit.

The Biography Kit is a two-part simulation of the process of preparing
and writing a biography. The first part of the kit provides for the creation
of all the raw materials *for* the biography; the second part focuses on the
writing *of* the biography from all the information amassed. Given that
students are never at a loss for imaginative contributions, and that projects
are more successful when students are personally engaged in classroom
decisions, the imaginary subject *they* create will no doubt be a continual
source of inspiration and amusement to all.

The class must initially determine the vital statistics of their make-
believe subject. The number of statistics will be equal to the number of
students participating, since each contributes a particular item for the
chronology of the subject. After establishing this framework, students then
turn to the task of embellishing it with details.

Since one of the first responsibilities of a biographer is to gather as
much information as possible, students must generate a mass of material

for the Biography Kit. Depending on available space, objects that the class has or can find to donate may be collected in boxes labeled with some organizational pattern. (If boxes can be stored from year to year, a record of who gave what can be marked on the lid of the box so that the box itself has a biography.) If each student contributes one item (e.g., an old trophy, a locket with an inscription, used ticket stubs), the subject will quickly take shape. Again, it is an opportunity for students to acquire vested interests in the welfare of the subject. Further, these items will trigger ideas for additional information, specifically created to enrich the subject's life.

Part 1 of the kit resembles, in many ways, the creation of a soap opera. Students are limited only by their imaginations; any twist in the narrative is encouraged provided it is substantiated by documentation. For example, scandals may be interjected. Newspaper articles can be written, then reproduced to look like actual clippings. Students can give, tape, and transcribe interviews with "friends" of the subject, using pre-pared questions of their own invention. Blank reports and certificates are handy resources for quick additional information. The general list of items at the end of this article should spark many additional ideas.

There is no danger of creating too much material. No doubt some objects will provoke more interest than others, but each represents some piece of the puzzle in reconstructing the life of the subject. Students must examine each item for its shape and content to determine whether it fits into the biography and if so, how. These materials developed spontane-ously lend a certain capriciousness to the skeletal narrative that is akin to the reality of our lives. Too, students should be impressed by the kind and quantity of documentation we are all in the process of gathering throughout our lives, for it is exactly those kinds of objects that we will surely include in the life of our make-believe subject. Once everybody's contribution has enjoyed some scrutiny, the business of writing the biography begins.

Part 2 of the kit switches focus from the creation of information about the subject to the creation of the biography. Initially the material should be arranged to provide a panorama of the subject's life, before being divided into chapters for writing. Each single part needs to fit with the preceding and following chapters, so goals for each section need to be set. The organizational pattern may follow numerous models, but for demon-stration purposes we will use five typical divisions: *background; child-hood; education; adult life;* and *death.* Chapter outlines should be posted on a panorama board so that problems posed early in the subject's life can be resolved in later chapters. This fulfills the need to coordinate single chapters so that they will dovetail with one another, unifying the biography.

Actual chapter assignments can be delegated according to time and needs and numbers. One class can prepare all the materials for part 1, and another class can write the biography. Or a single student can use the kit for an independent study, doing all five parts; or five students can do a chapter apiece; or five groups of five students each can work on isolated chapters. The last grouping is the most challenging collaborative effort, because the process of writing a biography requires developed decision-making skills. Students are called upon to inspect again each piece of evidence and to decide which items are most important to the biography. Here students are constantly evaluating not only what aspects of the subject's life would appeal to a diverse reading audience but also what aspects deserve emphasis, shrouding, illumination, interpretation.

No matter how the research assistants are organized, every biography should be published, dedicated at a group reading, and reviewed by a local critic. An autograph party for all the authors and their invited guests would be an appropriate ending to a unit using the Biography Kit.

The success of the Biography Kit depends on how imaginative students are about the subjects they create; both students and subjects must come alive. Subjects must be unusual, heroes who can take all the laughter and abuse generated; the personalities that emerge must be able to be forever forgiving of the abuse and be able to respond with humor to the narrative. In short, they must be unforgettable subjects, ghosts who haunt our classrooms and are later recalled with affection and respect, subjects worthy of our biographies.

Suggested Items That Can Be Collected

Background

Family: Bible
         tree
         portraits
         reunion description
         recipe box
Heirlooms/antiques
Citizenship papers

Childhood

Birth: certificate
       announcement
Baptism papers
Baby book

Stuffed animal
Posters
Trophies, medals, awards, pennants
Drawings, poems, stories
Favorite article of clothing
Correspondence: from summer camp
                with penpals
                with grandparents
Medical records
Childhood library
Record albums
Hobby collections
Handmade crafts and gifts
Diaries, journals
Religious objects

Education

Diploma
Class schedule
Class picture
Yearbook
Literary magazine
School newspaper
Curriculum vitae/résumé
Letters of recommendation
Report cards
Souvenirs: T-shirt
        mug
        class ring
        dance program
Letters from roommates/classmates
Programs or ticket stubs from plays, concerts, tours, athletic events

Adult Life

Scrapbook
Shopping list
Appointment book
Diary

Address book
Medical bills
IRS accounts
Check stubs
Passport
Travel journals
Letters
Will
Insurance policy
Favorite: hat
       pipe
       watch
       purse
       coat
       jewels
Military: papers
       uniform
       medals
Wedding: album
       service/ceremony
       invitation
       guest list
       menu
       certificate
       newspaper account
Mementos of first: car
            pet
            house
Ledger of household expenses
Cards: membership
     credit
     license
     Social Security

Death

Certificate
Obituary
Testimony
Memorials

Bibliography

Bibliographies

Alm, Richard S., ed. *Books for You.* New York: Washington Square Press, 1964.

Arbuthnot, May Hill, and Dorothy M. Brodrick. *Time for Biography.* Glenview, Ill.: Scott, Foresman & Co., 1969.

Butman, Alexander, Donald Reis, and David Sohn, eds. *Paperbacks in the Schools.* New York: Bantam Books, 1963.

Carlsen, G. Robert. *Books and the Teenage Reader.* New York: Bantam Books, 1967.

Christensen, Jane, ed. *Your Reading: A Booklist for Junior High and Middle School Students.* Urbana, Ill.: NCTE, 1983.

Committee on College Reading. *Good Reading.* New York: New American Library, 1954.

Donelson, Kenneth, and Alleen Pace Nilsen. *Literature for Today's Young Adults.* Glenview, Ill.: Scott, Foresman & Co., 1980.

Ellis, Webb, ed. *A Teacher's Guide to Selected Literary Works.* New York: Dell, 1969.

Small, Robert C., Jr., ed. *Books for You: A Booklist for Senior High Students.* Urbana, Ill.: NCTE, 1982.

Tway, Eileen, ed. *Reading Ladders for Human Relations.* Urbana, Ill.: ACE and NCTE, 1981.

White, Mary Lou, ed. *Adventuring with Books: A Booklist for Preschool-Grade 6.* Urbana, Ill.: NCTE, 1981.

Workman, Brooke. *Writing Seminars in the Content Area: In Search of Hemingway, Salinger, and Steinbeck.* Urbana, Ill.: NCTE, 1983.

Works Consulted

Angelou, Maya. *I Know Why the Caged Bird Sings.* New York: Bantam Books, 1970.

Arbuthnot, May Hill, and Dorothy M. Brodrick. *Time for Biography.* Glenview, Ill.: Scott, Foresman & Co., 1969.

Beach, Richard. *Writing About Ourselves and Others.* Urbana, Ill.: ERIC and NCTE, 1977.

Bloom, Benjamin, et al. *Taxonomy of Educational Objectives: Handbook 1: Cognitive Domain.* New York: Longman, 1977.

Booth, Wayne C. *The Rhetoric of Fiction.* Chicago: University of Chicago Press, 1961.

Christensen, Francis, and Bonniejean Christensen. *Notes Toward a New Rhetoric: Nine Essays for Teachers.* New York: Harper & Row, 1978.

Corbett, Edward P. J. *Classical Rhetoric for the Modern Student,* 2d ed. New York: Oxford University Press, 1971.

Donelson, Kenneth, and Alleen Pace Nilsen. *Literature for Today's Young Adults.* Glenview, Ill.: Scott, Foresman & Co., 1969.

Evans, Ronald V. "The Monomyth and the Teaching of Literature." *Arizona English Bulletin* 24, no. 1 (October 1981): 18–25.

Gibson, Walker. *Tough, Sweet, and Stuffy: An Essay on Modern American Prose Styles.* Bloomington: Indiana University Press, 1977.

Guerin, Wilfred, et al. *A Handbook of Critical Approaches to Literature.* New York: Harper & Row, 1979.

Kohlberg, Lawrence. "Moral Stages and Moralization: The Cognitive-Developmental Approach." In *Moral Development and Behavior: Theory, Research and Social Issues,* ed. Thomas Lickona (New York: Holt, Rinehart & Winston, 1976), 34–35.

Leeming, David Adams. *Mythology: The Voyage of the Hero.* New York: Harper & Row, 1980.

Lillard, Richard G. *American Life in Autobiography: A Descriptive Guide.* Palo Alto, Calif.: Stanford University Press, 1956.

Malmstrom, Jean, and Janice Lee. *Teaching English Linguistically: Principles and Practices for High School.* Englewood Cliffs, N.J.: Prentice-Hall, 1971.

Parr, Susan Resneck. *The Moral of the Story: Literature, Values and American Education.* New York: Teachers College Press, 1982.

Pechter, Mark, ed. *Telling Lives: The Biographer's Art.* Washington, D.C.: New Republic Books, 1979.

Pratt, Annis. *Archetypal Patterns in Women's Fiction.* Bloomington: Indiana University Press, 1977.

Reimer, Joseph, Diana Pritchard Paolitto, and Richard H. Hersh. *Promoting Moral Growth: From Piaget to Kohlberg,* 2d ed. New York: Longman, 1983.

Sandburg, Carl. *Abe Lincoln Grows Up.* New York: Harcourt Brace, 1926.

Smith, Sidonie. *Where I'm Bound: Patterns of Slavery and Freedom in Black American Autobiography.* Westport, Conn.: Greenwood Press, 1974.

Stillman, Paul. *Introduction to Myth.* New Rochelle, N.Y.: Hayden Book Co., 1977.